DOING
LEADERSHIP
DIFFERENTLY

J.M.W. TURNER, British 1775–1851, *The Red Rigi* 1842, watercolour, 30.5 × 45.8 cm, Felton Bequest, 1947, National Gallery of Victoria, Melbourne

Leadership is an idea available for us to shape and re-form. Art, and aesthetic pleasure in art, invite us to see new possibilities in leadership. I have come to see *The Red Rigi* as a picture about leadership— about Turner as an amazing leader, foreshadowing new ways to portray the world, making available to us transcendant and powerful meanings in colour and light.

Amanda Sinclair

DOING
LEADERSHIP
DIFFERENTLY

*Gender, Power and Sexuality
in a Changing
Business Culture*

Amanda Sinclair

MELBOURNE UNIVERSITY PRESS

Melbourne University Press
an imprint of Melbourne University Publishing Ltd
PO Box 278, Carlton South, Victoria 3053, Australia
info@mup.unimelb.edu.au
www.mup.com.au

First published 1998
Reprinted 1999
Revised edition 2005

Designed by Sandra Nobes
Typeset in Malaysia by Seng Teik Sdn. Bhd. in 11½ point Perpetua
Printed in Australia by McPhersons Print Group

National Library of Australia Cataloguing-in-Publication entry

Sinclair, Amanda, 1953–   .
    Doing leadership differently: gender, power and sexuality
    in a changing business culture.
    [2nd edn.]
    Bibliography.
    Includes index.
    ISBN 0 522 85149-5.

    1. Leadership. 2. Women executives. 3. Organizational change. I. Title.
658.4092

Publication of this work was assisted by a special publications grant from the University of Melbourne.

CONTENTS

PREFACE TO THE REVISED EDITION

When *Doing Leadership Differently* was first published, one of the first reactions I received was to the preface. I had begun it by reflecting on my pregnant stomach and wondering whether there was still sufficient impetus—in me and in the surrounding context—to justify launching a major new critique of leadership. A colleague who teaches leadership had recommended his students read the book: he reported back to me that some of them found this reference 'a turn-off' and 'inappropriate'. Books about leadership are not supposed to be personal (unless of course they are in the genre of 'Memoirs of the CEO . . .'). They are certainly not supposed to introduce gender and sexuality—and position the author's gender (as female and pregnant)—so prominently in the discussion.

This reaction provides a small taste of one of the flaws in the theory and practice of leadership that the book sets out to illuminate and redress. The leadership canon has effectively rendered invisible the gendered and sexual dimensions of much contemporary leadership practice. This rendering is not accidental. By making these dimensions of dominant leadership invisible, they become undiscussable and beyond critique, challenge and change.

I begin the preface to the revised edition with this story because it demonstrates how traditional views erect boundaries about what should, and shouldn't, be part of the study of leadership. The subtitle of the book, *Gender, Power and Sexuality in a Changing Business Culture*, indicates my conclusion that to reveal new directions in leadership, some of these traditional boundaries should be transgressed. Aspects of leadership that have been hidden or ignored should be in the foreground, not on the sidelines, of our analyses.

In *Doing Leadership Differently* I maintain that leadership as a concept has failed us. Our understandings of leadership have become captured by models from business that perpetuate heroic stereotypes and narrow measures of success, while alienating significant parts of the population who might otherwise seek to make a leadership contribution. The central argument of the book is that opening ourselves to some new thinking about leadership is long overdue and will benefit all of us: leaders and followers, men and women, people in organizations and societies.

In 2004, despite large amounts of research and some innovation in practice, I believe that the need to do leadership differently has gathered even more urgency. The impact and power of leadership exercised in corporate and managerial settings has grown, yet that same leadership appears to have become more immune to challenge or substantive change.

Increasingly, an ideology of leadership has evolved which portrays leadership as an enlightened force that frees people to deliver their potential, but fails to mention that this is in the interests of profit for the already privileged in wealthy countries—the managers and owners of capital. The language of enlightenment, democracy and freedom is seamlessly connected to agendas that are self-interested and futures that are commodified and enslaved. Without a qualm the language of the high moral ground is annexed. We are encouraged to 'unleash our passion and imagination', 'to create rule-breaking strategies', to 'free talent and capital', 'to challenge orthodoxies' but for what? Making the company great? And the lessons of leadership are presented as generic. They may have been honed in corporations but are as applicable in schools and universities, community and public sector organizations.

Leadership in this form shapes economics, politics, international affairs in new and pervasive ways. The fallout of the various corporate scandals that rocked America, Australia and various European nations in the late twentieth and early twenty-first century have not produced radical reassessments of the job of leadership. Indeed, it has been deeply alarming to watch various leaders—CEOs, managers and directors of all nationalities—step largely unscathed from the wreckage of their corporations with barely a backward glance of contrition. The lesson seems to be that they have not learned any lessons.

While one question might be what is it about the psyche of leaders that creates an immunity to reflection, perhaps a more important question is why leadership scholars too often collude in rewarding narcissism with sycophancy.

Performances of leadership, in Australia and in many other countries tilting towards globalised business models, have become captive of an ideology of leadership. I make the case in *Doing Leadership Differently* that the dominant archetype of the great corporate leader has embedded assumptions about the necessity of a heroic, heterosexual masculine performance, yet those assumptions are rarely inspected or assessed for their usefulness. They have a mythic power which resists deconstruction. Some readers of the first edition mistook the emphasis on gender and assumed *Doing Leadership Differently* was a book about women's leadership. Though I do believe much can be learned from women's leadership, this reading misses a crucial point—leadership, as traditionally enacted, delivers a privileged masculinity. Understanding this symbiotic connection is the first step in envisaging different paths to leadership.

In the ensuing years since I wrote *Doing Leadership Differently* my research and work have revealed many examples of people finding new paths to leadership. Analyses of gender, sexuality and power in leadership continue to provide a rich and fertile platform from which to 'see' leadership with fresh eyes. Working with men and women managers and professionals to map the ways in which a masculine and heroic performance comes to be accepted as synonymous with leadership yields instantly recognisable insights. All sorts of audiences readily list the rituals associated with this kind of leadership—the capacity to work long hours (assuming a partner is able to pick up family responsibilities), willingness to travel at short notice, client rituals which revolve around sports such as football or golf. By identifying these phenomena as social constructions, and charting the ways an industry or profession has defined particular performances as leadership (and marginalised others as lower status), people take the first step in unshackling themselves from the thrall of imprisoning ideas of 'leadership'. For all those who have struggled to 'deliver' against this archetype of leadership, simply seeing and naming its undiscussed hegemony is liberating. Recognising that one's own leadership doesn't have to conform to this (indeed, perhaps is more valuable if it doesn't) is more powerful still.

For men and women in organisations, being different as leaders means asking what their leadership work is for, and whose agenda or interests are advanced by it. It involves standing up for work that is valuable and important, and insisting on doing it in a reflective and compassionate way, not simply capitulating to imperatives generated by an overpowering boss, truculent client or invented sense of urgency. Leadership of this kind risks the individual being scape-goated, being singled out as 'not a team player' or not 'on board' with the interests of the organization. Yet, in a wider sense, taking such a position is exactly what leadership is often about.

Doing leadership differently also means bringing the whole self to the job, not living in camouflage. This can include many things: asserting values that are important but have been crushed under the weight of other priorities, bringing other parts of the self to the role, the sexual and gendered parts, the trusting and generous parts. Identity theory recognises that we have multiple selves and the argument here is not to go searching for and living the one authentic identity that is you. Nor is it to split the work self from the 'real' self and impose strict boundaries to ensure the two never meet. Rather it is to recog-nise that it is unhealthy physically and psychologically, emotionally and spiritually, to be locked into a life that compromises too much of what is important to us. Doing leadership differently means being thoughtful about the presence we want to be and the impact we want to have, at work and in society.

Among scholars and students of leadership, I still see too much of what I call the 'track down the truth about leadership, trap it and train in it' approach. In a discipline with a million books and articles paying homage to leadership, the task of today's scholarship is surely to ask deeper questions about why one would want to foster it. By advocating leadership, we can often find ourselves lined up with the status quo, helping to shore up the voices of the powerful and increase their capacity to control the lives of the powerless. Even those of us who seek to adopt a more critical perspective can end up infusing leadership with more mystique, rendering the canon we are seeking to critique more robust. Leadership should never be simply accepted as an unexamined good. Arguments for leadership always require accompanying analyses of power and control.

In my own writing, I have become increasingly disaffected with traditional methods of investigating and writing about leadership: the heroic stories of CEOs who turn around companies. The inevitable lists of actions and prescriptions help to support the fantasy that leadership is a commodity that can be bottled and bought by the smartest bidder.

So, now I aim to put the personal story back into leadership, to reflect about my own experiences as leader and follower, to write in language that does not disown the emotional complexity of the relationship we all have with leadership.

When I wrote this book I advocated that we should see leadership as an idea available for us to shape and re-form. I urged readers not to shy away from taking ownership of leadership, not to cede the leadership territory to a single band of leadership scholars or retired CEOs pushing barrows. I am not sure how well I was doing this myself, back in 1998.

Now, I view leadership as the most important part of the work that we all do and the influence we have in our lives. There is leadership—potentially—in most actions and sometimes it is the most common of actions in which we can exercise extraordinary leadership. Leadership is work that serves valuable purposes, be those purposes to help people around us to grow, to adapt, to support, to learn, to do new things, to take responsibility, to take risks which unveil formerly unseen possibilities. My own capacity to recognise leadership in new places—in others as well as myself—has increased, along with my willingness to go out on a limb to advocate it.

I would have liked the picture at the front of this book to be on the cover of *Doing Leadership Differently*, but my publishers thought differently, so we compromised by putting it inside near the cover. I wanted this lovely image by J. M. W. Turner, *The Red Rigi*, for a mixture of personal, poetic and imaginative reasons. I first came across it as part of an exhibition of Turner's works that my late brother, Michael Lloyd, curated. The exhibition coincided with the last months of Michael's life. He taught me the beauty in this picture.

But I have also come to see *The Red Rigi* as a picture about leadership—about Turner as an amazing leader, foreshadowing impressionism in new ways of portraying the world, not sticking to realistic mirroring but making available to us transcendant and powerful meanings in colour and light. There is also leadership presented in the content of the painting: in the beautiful floating rigi, an immense spiritual presence with both strength and lightness; in the vast pool of the lake and its fading reflections; in the shimmering shaft of light descending from the clouds and making for the viewer the gentle connection between the ordinariness of human activity and a larger order of things. Art, and the aesthetic pleasure in art, can invite us into new possibilities in leadership.

I hope you enjoy this new edition of *Doing Leadership Differently*, and I hope it inspires you to take your own practice of leadership to beautiful and surprising places.

Amanda Sinclair
2004

ACKNOWLEDGEMENTS

This book is for the women and men who are doing leadership differently. I wish to thank particularly the interviewees—the eleven men and twelve women who shared their lives and experiences of organisations and leadership. The women are Noel Waite, Negba Weiss-Dolev, Yvonne Von Hartel, Shirley Randell, Jan Roberts, Esther Ruberl, Deidre Mason, Merran Kelsall, Rhonda Galbally, Jacqueline Gillespie, Jenny Brice and Rita Avdiev. The men are listed in *Trials at the Top*.

I also want to thank all those who have talked with me, offered anecdotes and dreams, difficulties and triumphs, slices of work and snatches of lives. They include many friends at the University of Melbourne and in organisations, particularly faculty, students and graduates of the Melbourne Business School. Working with Noel Waite and the participants in her Ultimate Steps Programmes in Melbourne and Sydney has helped me shape my ideas and provided reassuring evidence from their experience of the significance of the issues I discuss in this book. Executive groups undertaking programmes at the Melbourne Business School and my consulting clients at Hewlett-Packard Australia and Esso Australia, among others, have been instructive in teaching me about teaching others— in areas of diversity, gender, sexuality and other traditionally taboo subjects in executive development. I am particularly grateful for the enthusiastic support of Fiona Krautil at Esso, Rose-Marie Todes at Hewlett-Packard and other members of the Inter-Company Network.

Many others, women and men, privately and in corporate settings, have offered anecdotes and insights which, I hope, gives richness and authenticity to the picture of leadership that has emerged.

Since the book was first published, I have received wonderful feedback from many students, executives and readers of all kinds who have drawn on its insights and tested the conclusions against their experiences. I wish to acknowledge these contributions to my unfolding ideas about leadership described in the preface.

In preparing the book for this reprint I would like to acknowledge the National Gallery of Victoria and the Felton Bequest for allowing me to reproduce *The Red Rigi* by J. M. W. Turner which appears in the front pages of the book and holds much significance for me (see my comments in the preface). I appreciate MUP's enthusiasm for re-printing the book, and Sybil Nolan's commitment to creating its new and attractive cover.

Finally, and again, I want to thank all the members of my family for being themselves and for their support of me—to Warwick, who uncomplainingly reads and improves (too many) drafts of my work; to my mother, Barbara Lloyd, who gave me her belief in words and love of ideas; and to my children, James, Amy, Huw and Charlie, who, remarkably, seem to find space in their lives to be genuinely and warmly interested in their mum's work.

1 WHY DO LEADERSHIP DIFFERENTLY?

Leadership, as a concept at least, has failed us. Despite the earnest efforts of business leaders and management writers to ennoble and dignify it, understandings of leadership have become cheapened by overuse. Leadership has been rendered impotent to deliver its promise.

There is an overwhelming need to reconstruct the concept of organisational leadership, to look for leadership in new places. In this book I argue that we can do so by reappraising leadership through the lens of gender and sexuality. Examining men's and women's experience of leadership reveals how traditional understandings of leadership have become exhausted—cynically exhorted, barren of meaning and unable to offer us hope. Exploring different approaches to the leadership task provides new insights and fresh purpose.

Leadership is a social construction—the product of the emotional and often unconscious needs, early experiences and group aspirations of the led, as well as the traits and skills of the leader. Understanding these symbolic and mythic origins of leadership helps to explain our insatiable, and so often disappointed, hunger for leadership, and why so few women are recognised as leaders.

Specifically I propose that there is a close but obscured connection between constructs of leadership, traditional assumptions of masculinity and a particular expression of male heterosexual identity. Theoretical formulations of leadership have lost meaning partially because of our failure to recognise this connection and move beyond it.

How are traditional notions of leadership faring in the internationalised and multicultural workplace ostensibly committed to equal opportunity? A vast management development industry has devoted itself to honing leadership skills. Yet there is little evidence that our notions of corporate leadership are changing to reflect or align with the shifting imperatives of a global marketplace. We are frequently warned that in these times of purportedly unprecedented change only those who innovate will survive. But our conceptions of leadership are locked in a time-warp, constrained by lingering arche-types of heroic warriors and wise but distant fathers. Stepping beyond the argument that leadership is a gendered construction, I will show how particular expressions of sexuality have always supported the enactment of leadership.

Why are so few women designated as organisational leaders? I will argue that we should not look simply to women to answer this question, or expect them to solve the problem of their troubling scarcity. Rather, the rarity of women in leadership roles is an oppor-tunity to re-appraise leadership—in theory and in practice.

Why are our expectations of leaders so resistant to change? And what does this reveal about the purposes of leadership? What are the experiences of leaders who are trying to lead differently? Is what they offer an ultimately unsatisfying and lesser leadership? If so, why? What does this mean for leadership in the new globally local (and locally global) multicultural millenium?

This book seeks to answer these questions by reporting findings from research, including my own on Australian organisational leaders, men and women. My exploration also draws on several bodies of theory—on leadership and organisational theory, particu-larly that relating to organisational culture; on feminism and research on women in society; on psychology and psychoanalytic theories of development; and on men and masculinity, an emerging sub-discipline which draws insights from sociology, gender and cultural studies as well as political theory.

We are still a long way from seeing equal numbers of female and male leaders, or indeed an understanding of leadership which gen-uinely takes gender into account rather than accepting male experi-ence of leadership as the norm. The reasons are deeply embedded in the way we interweave our understandings of leadership, assump-tions about masculinity, womanliness and sexuality. I argue for greater recognition, in the analysis of leadership, of historical and cultural forces. Much of the debate about directions of leadership has relied on arguments of economic imperatives and the language of the markets. This is to fail to understand the purposes that leadership has always served. Predictably, this debate has not helped us to explain why the leaders of large Australian organisations remain very largely male and of Anglo-Celtic origins.

How does my approach differ from recent Australian books which traverse some of the same territory—for example, Eva Cox's *Leading Women* (1996), James Sarros' *Leadership* (1996), and Susan Mitchell's *The Scent of Power* (1996)? I am trying to bridge a gap between academic writing and popular commentary on leadership, gender and sexuality. It was very clear from the response to *Trials at the Top* (Sinclair 1994) that practitioners, managers and executives had an appetite for locating in a wider framework the origins and meanings of their day-to-day experience. *Doing Leadership Differently* integrates the theoretical thinking which I have found most innovative and elucidating with the findings from my research and anecdotal material, including published interviews and profiles. I want to show how new connections between leadership and power, gender and sexuality are played out. I also want to share with a wider audience the individual experimentation and innovation in leadership practice that I have encountered in my teaching and research.

Workforce Diversity and Leadership Homogeneity

The Australian workforce is the among the 'most culturally and linguistically diverse of any workforce in the world' (Office of Multicultural Affairs 1993: 1). Over 85 per cent of workplaces contain more than four different nationalities, with 28 per cent containing more than eleven nationalities.

The ethnicity and geographic origin of Australia's workforce has undergone dramatic change in the last few decades. There have been large increases of workers born in Asia (particularly Vietnam, China, Taiwan and Hong Kong), in South America, in parts of Europe (such as Yugoslavia) and in parts of the Indian subcontinent (such as Sri Lanka). In contrast to earlier decades when immigrant workers fitted into existing institutions and conformed to traditional patterns of work, they are increasingly influencing the very structure and philosophy of management. In Melbourne and Sydney these communities are often large enough to build distinctive entrepreneurial cultures and areas of management expertise.

Turning to changes in the gender composition and family structures of the working population, 42 per cent of the Australian labour force are now women—one of the few groups whose rate of employment is continuing to climb. Women comprise close to 50 per cent of graduates in business, law and related disciplines and are now, consistently, the better academic performers (Poole and Langan-Fox 1997). Women's careers and lives are undergoing profound change. In Australia, two-thirds of women are back to work within eighteen months of childbearing, in the United States two-thirds are back within six weeks (this may well not be a model we wish to emulate).

By the end of the century, 20 per cent of women of childbearing age will not have children and many will have decided not to for career and job-related reasons. Women born in the 1960s are twice as likely as their mothers never to have children. At the same time, 15 per cent of all families are single-parent ones and, with an ageing population, many employees have elder-care responsibilities.

Managers and leaders are seeking to get the best from a workforce that is almost unrecognisable from those of twenty or thirty years ago. Traditional stereotypes of 'the breadwinner' are almost bound to be wrong. The markets that managers are serving have correspondingly reflected huge changes. To be successful, managers need now to have an appetite to understand and cater for great variety in what people want.

However, this high degree of diversity in the workforce is not reflected in the characteristics and experience of executives and leaders in Australia. In work done for the Bureau of Immigration, Multicultural and Population Research, Ian Watson finds that 'NESB (non-English speaking background) immigrants . . . face a glass door which blocks their entry into the managerial labour force' (1996: ix). This is not a matter of inadequate education or experience—indeed NESB managers are more highly educated than their Anglophone counterparts. Watson explains the obstacles facing NESB managers using Bourdieu's (1977; 1978) notion of 'cultural capital'—it is the informal norms, language, skills and habits which open doors and facilitate movement into the managerial job market. 'Simply lacking the right cultural capital can exclude an overseas-born manager' (Watson 1996: 33).

Australia is not alone in the trend towards workforce diversity while retaining management and leadership homogeneity, although it can certainly be argued that Australia is showing less propensity for change than some other countries. In the United States, for example, the Glass Ceiling Commission concludes from its five-year study that

> America's vast human resources are not being fully utilized because of glass-ceiling barriers . . . Over half of all Masters degrees are now awarded to women, yet 95 per cent of senior level managers of the top *Fortune* 1000 and 500 service companies are men. Of them, 97 per cent are white (1995: 6).

Similarly, Karston finds that 'Regardless of how the percentages are calculated, less than 5% of senior managers in major U.S. firms are women' (1994). This low level persists despite demographic changes and evidence that the average annualised return on investment of companies which don't discriminate against women is more than double that of companies with a poor record of hiring and promoting women (Glass Ceiling Commission 1995).

In the United Kingdom, Davidson and Cooper estimated that in 1987 only 1–2 per cent of senior executives were women; by 1992 the proportion had not significantly increased, indeed there was some evidence of plateauing. Collinson and Hearn (1996) cite further evidence showing the number of female managers had declined by the early 1990s, that they continued to be paid substantially less and were more likely to have resigned. And across diverse Asian countries, Adler concludes that women's 'near absence from executive positions renders them almost invisible' (1993: 4).

In Australian organisations, particularly private companies, the proportion of women in executive positions is as low, if not lower, than in comparable industrialised economies. Drawing together the findings from her own research and a comprehensive overview of other Australian studies, Still (1993) finds evidence that the proportion of senior executives who are women, far from showing a steady increase, may be declining. In her study of 124 of Australia's

'Top 1000' companies, Still found that the proportion of senior managers who were women declined from 2.5 per cent in 1984 to 1.3 per cent in 1992. An International Labour Organisation study cited by Still judged that Australia has the lowest percentage of female managers among industrialised countries and is showing a relatively slow rate of increase.

In another survey of 243 of Australia's largest employers, Smith and Still (1996) found that 93 per cent of overseas posts were filled by men. Companies retained a lingering belief that men were more suitable overseas appointments, despite women's superior qualifications and research which shows that women are at least as likely to be successful as men in overseas appointments (Adler and Izraeli 1988).

The proportion of women senior executives in the Australian public sector is higher—around 16 per cent at the federal level, and in some states the proportion is a little higher. Although these achievements are welcome, they follow over a decade of affirmative action and equal employment opportunity legislation.

If we turn to the top jobs—that of CEO or managing director in the private sector, or departmental head, secretary or vice chancellor in the public sectors—then the proportion of women is minute indeed. At the Board level, women now comprise around 10 per cent of director positions among America's largest 500 companies (Dobrzynski 1996). A recent study of 596 top Australian companies by Egan Associates painted a poorer picture: 2.7 per cent of directors are women and a small group of women hold multiple positions. Only 16 per cent of companies had at least one woman on their Board (Carruthers 1997).

Even in the United States observers are cautious about the more positive signs of increasing female representation on Boards. The rate of increase has slowed; only 23 of the 500 companies had three or more women on the Board, and the pool of potential senior executives from which executive directors are recruited remains minute and not noticeably growing. These trends are mirrored in the United Kingdom where the rate of change is 'moribund' (Holton 1995). Despite growth in numbers of female directors in the top 200 United Kingdom companies to 4 per cent, with a few exceptions women fill non-executive roles and only 1 per cent are executive directors.

Perhaps even more concerning than absolute numbers is the lack of evidence of any substantial and sustained increase in women's representation at the top of organisations. This is despite significant expansion in the pool of women with appropriate training and experience from which appointments might be made. Also, various studies of the expansion and success of women-run small businesses provide evidence of women's financial, management and leadership skills. Increasingly, Australian small business owners are women. Women start around 70 per cent of new businesses and are predicted to own 50 per cent of small businesses by 2000. They currently create about half the private-sector jobs. In the United States, women own over one-third of all private firms with a growth rate almost double that of other businesses.

And the evidence from Australia, France, the United Kingdom and elsewhere indicates that women run their organisations better. A New Zealand study found that small businesses run by women have a success rate at the end of the first year of 85 per cent compared to 50 per cent for male-run businesses (Sarney 1997). A study of 22 000 French firms found that those run by women were twice as profitable and growing twice as fast as those run by men (Hunter and Reid 1996).

These statistics indicate chronic under-utilisation of the pool of Australia's leadership and management talent, particularly evident in large organisations. The figures also suggest that the legislative measures introduced have barely melted the tip of the problem which, like the proverbial iceberg, has a depth and scale we have yet to comprehend. (See Still 1993 and Smith and Hutchinson 1995 for further summaries of Australian data).

Just as society's mix of genders is not represented in leadership, neither is the diverse, multicultural and multilingual nature of the workplace. Nor is that diversity reflected in the experience of most corporate decision-makers. Despite Australia's location within the Asia–Pacific region and its history of high levels of immigration, the statistics suggest that the management and leadership of Australian organisations is much more homogeneous than either its workforce or its market (domestic and international). There are, in addition, studies which provide further evidence of an insularity and a poor record of innovation in business processes. In contrast to some other

countries comparable in terms of industrialisation, the evidence indicates the existence of some peculiarly Australian obstacles to the
diversification of leadership.

Why Leadership has Resisted Change

Whatever else it is remembered for, the report of the Industry
Taskforce on Leadership and Management Skills, *Enterprising Nation*
(1995), will probably continue to be most often quoted for its assessment of the quality of Australia's management as being seventeenth
out of twenty-two top industrial nations. David Karpin, Chair of the
Industry Taskforce, argued that the failure to fully and innovatively
utilise diversity in the Australian workforce is a major contributing
factor to the mediocre performance of Australia in world competitiveness and management quality. He said that 'Only by entrench-
ing diversity will employees be optimally equipped to deal with the
competitive challenges expected of them by the international
marketplace and by the Australian community' (1994: 69)

One of the most frequent diagnoses of the causes of resistance to
innovation and change rests on a distinction between managers and
leaders. For example, *Enterprising Nation* characterises old-style
managers and new-style leaders/enablers, bluntly labelling old-style
managers as 'the problem'. Senior managers from the past are male,
of Anglo-Celtic background, started at the bottom of their organisation and had on-the-job management training, had a local focus in
one Australian state and had travelled once overseas (to England),
worked with established competitors, had paternalistic views of
workforces and worked in a stable environment.

The report prophesied (with a high degree of either optimism or
idealism) that senior managers of the future will be male or female,
with a wide range of ethnic backgrounds. They will have graduate and
postgraduate qualifications, wide-ranging careers and a global focus,
and will travel regularly, managing workforces in more than one
country and in both regulated and de-regulated economies, share
information, delegate heavily and work in an environment typified by
rapid change.

Certainly the characterisation of existing senior managers is
instantly recognisable. But they are not managers of the past; they are

still prominent in many Australian companies. Simply identifying the changes which *should* occur in leadership will not create that change. Instead we need to understand how it is that leadership has remained highly homogeneous, despite broad social, economic and workforce pressures to become more diverse. To answer this question, I will examine, in Chapter 2, the purposes leadership serves.

To understand leadership in the Australian business culture, to understand who becomes a leader and who does not, we need to look much deeper and wider than at individual characteristics. We need to recognise the force of images and icons that are deeply planted in the psyche of Australian business cultures and are resistant to the simple logic of workforce demographics or the economic imperatives of globalisation.

The Research

The ideas presented here are based on interviews with twelve senior executive women, in addition to the interviews with eleven male chief executives for *Trials at the Top* (Sinclair 1994).

To achieve 'a matched sample' of women, the ideal in empirical research, we would have had to find and interview female chief executives of companies similar in size and scope to the original group of eleven male chief executives. This, of course, is an impossible brief given the small population of women at senior levels of Australian private corporations. In a 1992 search of the thousand-odd companies listed on the Australian Stock Exchange, Professor Leonie Still found only seven female chief executives and seven female chairpersons (most held both positions) (Bagwell 1992). The Women Chiefs of Enterprise organisation, with a broad definition of 'chiefs', has a larger membership, from which we drew some of our interviewees.

The sample of twelve women includes those either at the top of companies—as chief executives, managing directors or directors— or in senior positions, evidenced by reporting to or being able to report to the CEO. Half of the women are chief executives or directors of small or medium-sized organisations. The other half are women working, or until recently working, within the top two to three layers of corporations, and who have had the ear of the chief executive if they need it.

When the original sample of male CEOs was chosen, two criteria were used: either they were very influential in the business community or they were known to have innovative views. Some qualified on both counts. In choosing the women, we also sought those whom we knew to be reflective about their own leadership and about the issues facing other women in similar roles.

Apart from this common quality of reflectiveness, there is considerable diversity in the sample of women. They are spread in age from the mid-thirties through to the fifties. Seven have children: in several cases they are young children requiring care, in other cases teenagers, and the remainder are independent though still important and influential in their mothers' lives. Seven are married or in stable relationships, with men or women, while others live alone though surrounded by a network of friends, family or both. The interviewees are listed in the Acknowledgements but I have used pseudonyms in the text to preserve confidentiality of quotes.

All the interviews were conducted around a set of open-ended questions covering three areas: the woman's experience of an executive environment; her perceptions of her career and leadership role; and questions about background, such as family and schooling. I offered respondents the choice of whether we started in the present and worked backwards or started with childhood and worked to the present. Most often, and rather to my surprise, it seemed easier to start with early experiences. Interviews ran for between 60 and 120 minutes with most closer to the latter. More than half were conducted in offices, theirs and mine, though a couple were held at their homes and out of hours—I gave them the choice of time and place.

I encouraged storytelling and narratives. Women generally found it quite difficult to talk about themselves, and themselves as leaders, describing it as 'feeling self-indulgent'. A smoother way to enter this territory was via critical incidents—both successes (where they felt they had handled a difficult situation or overcome significant resistance) and failures. Initially, talk of childhood was tentative, but many seemed to enjoy the unexpected opportunity to revisit early lives and see some connection between the girl, the young woman and the person they had become.

All interviews were transcribed. In reproducing segments of transcript, an ellipsis (. . .) indicates that some comments have been left out. Many of the 'umms', laughter and pauses are included, where they convey important things about the speaker's voice, level of comfort or uncertainty in retelling an incident. Italics indicate emphasis by the interviewee.

Rather than quote several women relaying similar sorts of experiences I have, particularly in Chapters 5, 6, 7 and 9, selected one representative quotation to stand for a number. Quotation from only one woman's experience should not be interpreted to mean that hers is a unique or isolated experience.

Although the interviews constitute the main body of data for this book, the insights presented are also informed by my ongoing work with managers and executives, men and women. The business of working with groups of managers and executives on matters of gender and diversity offers a rich pool of data. I have presented and discussed the issues advanced in this book to a range of audiences with varying gender balances: all male, all female, predominantly male and predominantly female. These are case studies in themselves, mapping the complex gender dynamics of how male and female audiences respond to situations where a woman has formal authority.

While the twenty-three interviews and supplementary data collection and discussion are the bases of the ideas I advance, this book should not be treated as reporting an empirical study. Because of the small sample size and the absence of corroborating organisational data, among other things, prescriptions cannot be drawn on the basis of these findings. At the same time, I hope that this combination of empirical data and the best of research findings from elsewhere will breathe new insights into that otherwise sadly debilitated construct of leadership.

My Motivation

My interest in how other women enact themselves when in leadership roles has inevitably been vigorously nurtured by my own experience. It has grown out of a sense of frustration at having, as I perceived it, to become somebody else in order to be taken seriously as myself. I feel I have had to hide much of the person I am in order to operate at a 'leadership' level. A retired male CEO who had read something of mine was unusually frank when he met me: 'I thought professors had to be old and big'. I have found myself defending my achievements as proof of leadership, aware that it rarely consoles those who sense a discrepancy between me and their image of leaders.

At the same time I have noted my own, and other women's, discomfort at fitting what we do and who we are into the leadership category. The first time my Director, Professor John Rose, talked of my 'leadership' in the Business School, I looked around to see who he was talking about. The connection of myself to leadership is not one that I make easily, as I suspect is the case for many women.

Unlike others, I do not lament this. I think it is good that women think about what their leadership is, who it serves, what it's for. The mantle of leadership sits uneasily, and I think this is a good check against Lord Acton's adage that power corrupts and absolute power corrupts absolutely. Bella Azbug, at the Beijing international women's conference in 1994, expressed this as an expectation that women would change the nature of power, rather than power changing women.

My experiences, as well as my research, have fuelled a commitment to illuminating the diversity of ways in which women express who they are, as women, in leadership roles. It involves making explicit the sexualised way leadership is defined. I hope it will also create space for women to be leaders in a much wider range of ways than at present. Instead of women struggling to assert their leadership against a norm of masculinism, they may be able to be themselves in the fuller sense, bringing their sexual as well as their intellectual selves to their leadership roles.

I called the book *Doing Leadership Differently* to highlight the enacted nature of leadership. In most contexts, leadership is presented as an unproblematic good, its value beyond debate. This book is not one which lists ways to be a leader. I wanted, in the title as elsewhere in the book, to maintain that leadership is not something that just *is*, to illuminate that leadership is always accomplished. Leadership is produced in words and actions, in images and artefacts, and it requires constant demonstration to be sustained. The process of accomplishing leadership requires the complicity of leader and led, a process that I argue is more ambivalent in the case of women leaders. While recognising that leadership is achieved through practices enacted within structures, the 'doing' part of the title also conveys the possibility of agency. I am referring here to my conclusion that people can make some choices about how they lead. They can bring more or less of themselves, they can experiment with self-revelation, with resistance, with trying to build new paths that others can follow. Finally, the title is intended to convey that society as a whole, as well as individuals within it, should be looking to 'do leadership differently'. Societies actively and collectively recognise and reproduce leadership. The onus is on us all, followers as well as leaders, to re-appraise our traditional constructs of leadership, looking at where they come from and how we want leadership to be in the future.

· · ·

Homogeneity in the characteristics of leadership, in an environment of dramatic change and with a workforce characterised by increasing diversity, is a major liability. Using sexualities and gender as a focus, I will examine how leadership has been enacted in Australian organisations and how that leadership has been experienced and emulated by others.

I do not take a particular position on the debate about whether men and women have different styles of leadership, although some of the research investigating this question is discussed. Any conclusion on whether women and men in their leadership are similar or different runs the risk of playing into the wrong hands. Pursuit of this path tends to leave underlying constructs of good leadership assumed and unexamined, the important questions overlooked. In seeking to prove or disprove such sex-based differences, it is easy to avoid addressing the really critical and challenging issues. Why does the phenomenon and concept of leadership so engross us? How and why do the romance and mystique, the magic and sex appeal of leadership persist? Yet why are we so regularly and irrevocably disenchanted by our leaders?

Despite my focus on gender and sexuality, this is not a book just about women. I argue that we should resist the long-standing habit of assuming that it is only women who have gender and that femaleness is the only sexuality. All leaders, male and female, enact gender and sexuality as part of leading. The second part of the book specifically attempts to unmask the important but often invisible interactions between masculinities and leadership. Through inspection of the way leadership has been linked to gender and sexualities in the past, and how this is changing, I hope to illuminate emerging forms of men and women doing leadership differently.

2

THE ABSENCE/INVISIBILITY
OF WOMEN IN LEADERSHIP

Few subjects have been so extensively researched as leadership. Since classical times scholars of history, politics and philosophy, and the ancestors of psychology, have sought to identify the ingredients and antecedents of leadership. Others (though fewer) have sought to understand the costs and the 'dark side' of leadership (for example, Denhardt 1981; Mant 1983; Kets deVries and Miller 1984; Gronn 1995). Leadership is considered in more articles and more citations than any other topic of management. Despite such prolific attention, 'no clear unequivocal understanding exists as to what distinguishes leaders from non-leaders . . . Never have so many labored so long to say so little' (Bennis and Nanus 1985: 4).

It is all the more striking in this context that the study of women and leadership is a new endeavour. As Nieva and Gutek note, 'leadership research has been concerned with men leading other men' (1981: 83). Although there has been passing attention given to men leading women, it has been men in charge of other men that has captured the imagination of researchers and biographers and spawned their fascination for military and sporting exemplars. The twin tests of leadership have surely been the capacity of men to stand above other men.

Why, despite the vast literature on leadership, has the study of women and leadership received so little attention? In exploring this question, I will examine theories of leadership and the relationships between women and leadership, gender and authority—specifically, three bodies of argument that purport to explain the absence of attention to women.

The first argument is that women are, for all intents and purposes, absent from leadership positions. The absence argument focuses on women, offering various reasons why they have not yet assumed leadership roles in significant numbers. I will look at why this explanation is so willingly and widely embraced by corporate Australia.

The second argument looks more deeply, suggesting that the way in which leadership has been defined, recognised and rewarded in organisations means that men are more likely to assume leadership roles. While women may not be absent in leadership roles, their contribution, because it looks different, may not be registered as leadership. Women's leadership, according to this view, is not absent, but rather is invisible to the conventional tests of leadership. These two explanations are popularised as the 'blame the victim' and the 'blame the system' explanations of women's apparent under-representation in leading positions.

Going a step further, I argue that the construct of leadership cannot simply be understood as a rational response to a well-articulated problem (see also Meindl *et al.* 1984). For leaders and followers, leadership is a mythical construction, fufilling emotional and spiritual needs. Ideas about who are leaders and what leadership is have strong cultural and collectively constructed roots. Deeply embedded, they are often taken for granted and not recognised or debated.

An aspiring leader cannot create leadership alone (Little 1985). Leadership is always the product of some collusion, whereby a band of supporters agrees that an individual, their leader, has what they need to lead them at a particular time. Leadership is therefore a social construction, a relationship that requires constant demonstration and legitimation. I propose the concept of leadership as an archetype in order to capture these collectively, but often unconsciously created, properties of leadership.

This alternative conception of leadership is developed throughout the book: that leadership and authority are constructed by audiences, by subordinates and superiors, by followers and peers. Because of a range of psychological, cultural and historic factors, starting with our experience of the first leader in our lives—our mothers—followers have been reluctant to imbue women with leadership qualities, even when they exhibit the same characteristics as men. Women will inevitably be seen to lead differently, and we need to build a new understanding which allows for this leadership.

The Absence Argument: Women-centred Explanations

The most common explanation for an absence of attention to women and leadership springs from a perception of few women in recognised positions of power and authority. The lack of research is thus justified on the basis that the phenomenon of female leaders does not really exist, or not in sufficient numbers to warrant serious attention.

One example of this explanation was expressed in a review of two books on female leaders: 'The reason why women have been neglected over the years seems for the most part obvious enough. Despite the occasional "achiever" . . . there are few women at decision-making levels' (Holton 1996: 57). As women increasingly gain the necessary qualifications and career experience, it is argued, we will then see more women in corporate leadership roles, who in turn become deserving of serious study.

This argument focuses on women to explain their absence. In an early and important article, Riger and Galligan identified two 'paradigms' which competed with one another in the 'women in management' literature (1980). The 'person-centred' or 'women-centred' explanation for the under-representation of women focuses on the characteristics, and shortcomings, of women. This reasoning observes a relative absence of women, and deduces that women must not possess the requisite attributes, training or experience to be leaders.

What I call the Absence Argument thus hinges on establishing that there are differences between men and women in what they potentially bring to leadership. A significant research industry has evolved aimed at testing whether men and women manage and lead differently. Part of this research agenda is built on the implicit assumption that because women are biologically and physiologically different, because they are 'programmed' to reproduce and nurture, they may not have the requisite toughness to take on leadership roles.

Some pioneering work done in the 1970s by Carol Gilligan, as well as work by Belenky and her colleagues (1986), has indeed argued that women tend to journey along different developmental and learning paths. This shows up in a stronger adult value placed on relationships and connectedness. These and other differences in male and female values and moral reasoning provided sufficient evidence, according to these researchers, to overturn the traditional devaluing of 'womens ways of knowing'. However, it alarmed other theorists because in the wrong hands this evidence can be, and has been, used to argue an inherent and essential unsuitability of women to fulfil leadership roles.

Research of sex differences should always be treated cautiously. In much of the management literature, findings of sex-based differences have been used as a pretext to school 'deficient' women in requisite toughness and assertiveness for leadership, advising them to consciously construct the networks and mentor relationships which men take for granted, and urging them to leave tendencies to nurture and 'love too much' at home. Women are counselled to improve their training and professional qualifications, and we are all encouraged to wait as the effects of improved education take effect in the workforce.

The Absence Argument has been popularly elaborated into an explanation known as 'the pipeline effect', which puts its faith in time and patience. The lack of women at the top has occurred, so the argument goes, because of past low recruitment of women at entry level, or the start of the pipeline. It is predicted that increasing numbers of female graduates and recruits into organisations will learn the implicit rules and requisites of leadership and gradually move through to executive ranks.

In my earlier book, *Trials at the Top* I outlined a four-stage process identified from interviews with chief executives. The four stages (see Table 1) represent the range of conceptualisations and explanations we encountered for the absence of women in senior management. The first three of these stages are all examples of the women-centred Absence Argument.

TABLE 1: PHASES OR TYPES OF EXECUTIVE CULTURE

Stage 1　**Denial: No Problem**
The absence of women from executive levels is not regarded as a problem or a core business issue.

Stage 2　**The Problem is Women**
Women's difference is seen as the problem and the solution lies in women learning how to adapt to (male) norms.

Stage 3　**Incremental Adjustment**
The organisation recognises a problem but sees that it will be solved by adjustments at the margin to allow access to individual women. One or two targetted appointments are made of women who already have a track record and are not seen as 'high risk'.

Stage 4　**Commitment to a New Culture**
The exclusion of women is recognised as a symptom of deeper problems requiring solutions focused on the existing culture. Initiatives examine the way things are currently done and the need for 'inside-out' change.

At Stage 1 the under-representation of women is 'not regarded as a key business issue'. The implication is that there is not a direct link between women's under-representation and the bottom-line. This is a surprisingly common view, expressed in companies for whom a large proportion of both their employees and their customers are women.

Stage 2 recognises a problem, but the problem is with women. Executives cite a whole range of individual experiences which reveal, for them, that the problem is with women:

> I really wanted a woman in this position and asked the head hunters to make sure they got me some for the short list. But they couldn't get any.

> There was a woman in South Australia who would have been perfect but we couldn't get her to move. She promised me she would talk to her husband but she came back that they didn't want to move.

Characteristic of Stage 2 is a tendency to generalise from experience with one women to all women. One CEO, for example, threw up his hands complaining, 'They just don't come back from maternity leave'. With some prompting, he admitted that the statistics showed that the vast majority of women did return from maternity leave and that the organisation retained more women graduates than men for the first four or five years after recruitment. This example illustrates a pattern of perception whereby women's maternity is construed as, and expected to be, 'a problem'. This then excuses the company's record of not keeping in touch with employees while on maternity leave, not providing some initial flexibility of hours and not ensuring that women return to an effective equivalent role.

In a study of thirteen public-sector CEOs in Western Australia, Helen Saunders (1996) found a broadly espoused commitment to increasing diversity in their management ranks. However, when asked why so few women were represented in senior levels, this group generally offered the women-centred, pipeline arguments characteristic of Stage 2:

> I don't think there's any prejudice at all. There are just not many females entering senior areas of government.

> We just don't attract women into the field. It's the nature of the work.

> In the past, women did not feature in our professional areas, and therefore, we have very few women in our organisation.

A number volunteered that the public sector lost women to the private sector, which could, they believed, attract women with better salaries. This is despite the statistics showing that the public sector has a better record at retaining and promoting women than does the private sector, and research evidence that women rarely rate high salaries as critical to their career decisions.

Examples of Stage 2 thinking can also be gleaned from the popular, as well as the academic, Press. In the case of a senior woman leaving a major Australian bank, the coverage of the reasons for her departure specifically selected women-centred explanations: that she wanted more time with her family. This was in spite of the evidence that she immediately took another job which involved more inter-state travel.

Stage 3 recognises the problem of women's under-representation, and senior male executives begin to take responsibility for solutions. However, the solutions remain focused on women. At this stage it is common for companies to invest heavily in a couple of high-profile Board or executive appointments. The unspoken expectation is that, once these appointments are made, the 'problem of women' can be delegated informally to these women. The problem will thus be solved by them, either explicitly or by their being role models to other women. The adjustments made are at the margins of the organisation's culture and the women appointed are typically those who are able to assimiliate into the dominant values and norms of the organisation.

I will examine the effect of these pressures on women to act as change agents for their organisations, as well as do their jobs, in Chapters 5, 6 and 7. It is not surprising that numbers of women appointed as directors or senior executives avoid or reject the in-clusion of women's issues in their portfolio of activities. Some see that taking on this role is a fast-track to marginalisation. Others insist on proving themselves in other aspects of the business before they take on any advocacy for women in the organisation. And some women insist on sharing with a senior male executive or director the role of expanding opportunities for senior women.

These examples of Stages 1 to 3 demonstrate how the Absence Argument and its attendant explanations are constructed—by the organisation and its spokespeople, by the Press and commentators—in ways which decision-makers find acceptable and consistent with their personal ideologies. Women are absent from senior levels because there are none who are qualified, who are willing to make the commitment, who are interested in the area, who are prepared to be sufficiently mobile, and so on.

The 'politics of optimism', as Blum and Smith have described this phenomenon, has also infected much of the women-in-management literature. The prescription of patience and focus on entry-level recruitment, combined with the 'implication that women need only change themselves to succeed' (Blum and Smith 1988: 531), has proved to be remarkably resilient, even though the statistics increasingly demonstrate that these solutions are based on a mis-diagnosis of the problem.

An array of evidence confirms that the problem is not one of no qualified and experienced women. Females now account for 54 per cent of undergraduates, with women outnumbering men in some business, law and arts/law courses. In information systems and accounting, there are substantial numbers of women graduating and results show women to be among the best graduates. In areas such as engineering, where a great deal of effort has been invested in en-couraging them, women now comprise over 13 per cent of students (30 per cent of chemical engineering graduates), with a steady growth rate of 5 per cent. It is clear that, over recent years, a sizeable pool of female graduates with appropriate training now exists. The most progressive companies have been able to recruit half or more of their entry-level professional intake from female graduates.

As the graduate profile has become more evenly balanced between men and women, but in the face of low promotion and longer term retention rates of women in organisations, some have argued that our understanding of the pipeline should be extended to include, in the first instance, 'on the job' training and experience; and in the second, postgraduate training such as a Master of Business Administration (MBA) qualification.

Yet women hold a steadily increasing proportion of postgraduate degrees awarded in business and related areas. In the United States women now hold over 40 per cent of all MBAs, although these statis-tics conceal that the MBA is still relatively gender-segregated—the higher the status of the MBA programme, the smaller the proportion of students likely to be women (Sinclair 1995a).

Corporate statistics show that a number of companies have been recruiting female graduates for long enough for them to acquire the necessary experience to be considered eligible for senior roles. The evidence is that the pipeline has failed to deliver the flow of women expected—that there are significant obstacles along the pipeline and that many women choose the exit option. The real reasons for their departure are often concealed, as neither the woman nor the company want them exposed. Practices go unchanged and senior company executives feel confirmed in their view that women are risky and expensive employment options, and are uncommitted to long-term careers.

In her work on female presidents and heads of state, Nancy Adler (1996) has recorded twenty-five women who have held such positions in recent times. As Adler notes, we need to look beyond the numbers to explain the pervasive and widely accepted myth that women cannot be successful global leaders. For example, the contributions of these women have often been marginalised in commentary which portrays them as agents of their fathers or husbands and therefore leaders by default or accident (interim leaders until the real business of leadership resumes).

In business, there is a similar process at work whereby women's performance in leadership roles is frequently redefined as something less than leadership. Most noteworthy for our purposes is the way these explanations have been embraced and perpetuated as a pervasive mindset among managers. Echoing widely expressed views, one male chief executive summed up the problem of under-representation in his company and where the solutions lay:

> Whether they [women] actually want to, or have the staying power, there is nothing much you can do. I don't think there is any real impediment to them except it's a male-dominated company and they have to be able to handle that.

The critical question to ask is why the Absence Argument and 'women-centred' explanations are so attractive and so tenaciously held, despite factual evidence to the contrary. Two reasons emerge from my research. Firstly, there is a desire for women to behave as women 'should'. That is, underlying these views and often expressed directly to the female managers concerned is the view that women should be at home with their children. Sometimes male executives volunteer that their own wives stayed at home until the children were at school or had left home. This perspective is often offered as a matter of protective concern, ostensibly seeking to safeguard the interests of the woman involved.

The second reason for the tenacity of the Absence Argument is that focusing on what women should, or should not, do obviates deeper and more challenging introspection and inspection of the organisation and its practices and policies. The 'women-centred' view enables executives to remain 'other-focused', to continue to have complete faith in company processes and norms and to conclude that it was the woman who failed to 'stand the heat of the kitchen'. This is, of course, a much more comfortable position that being 'self-focused' or asking, for example, whether the reason that there is no willing pool of women applying for jobs might be that the company has a poor reputation as an employer of women.

In summary, Australian organisations and executives continue to exhibit a tenacious embrace of the 'women-centred' view—that women are the problem and that women must provide the solution to their under-representation. I propose a need to look beyond the Absence Argument as an explanation for a lack of theorising about women and leadership. Recent work has demonstrated that the absence of attention to women as leaders may have more to do with the way in which concepts of leadership have been defined and recognised in organisations, on the one hand, and theorised in research, on the other. In these terms, the problem of absence is better conceptualised as a problem of invisibility—that is, that women's leadership has not been recognised as leadership within the largely male-constructed canon of leadership theory (Sinclair 1995b).

The Invisibility Argument: Construct-centred Explanations

A substantial body of research concludes that men and women do not behave very differently as leaders (for example Powell 1988). Women, according to this perspective, have 'what it takes' to lead. This evidence, along with the shortcomings of 'woman-centred' explanations, encourages us to pursue other hypotheses to explain the neglect of women and leadership.

One hypothesis has been pioneered and developed in the empirical work of Virginia Schein and her colleagues. Their argument is not that men and women manage or lead differently, but that they are perceived differently. Summed up as 'think manager–think male', Schein's research (1973; 1975; 1996) demonstrates that effectiveness as a manager is attributed not exhibited, and is attributed more readily to men, by both men and women. Women exhibiting the same behaviours as men are not judged as equally authoritative or as having requisite management characteristics (Nieva and Gutek 1981; for a summary of more recent studies see Wilson 1995).

In a number of comprehensive studies, Eagly and her colleagues (1990; 1992) have tested gender differences in leadership style and evaluations of male and female leaders. They conclude firstly that gender differences in preferred leadership do exist but are hard to capture in field studies because of the effects of socialisation and pressures on women to conform to organisational norms. Secondly Eagly, like Schein, found clear evidence that female leaders exhibiting the same behaviours as males will be more negatively evaluated. Devaluation was most pronounced 'when leadership was carried out in stereotypically masculine styles . . . when leaders occupied male-dominated roles and when the evaluators were men' (1992: 2).

Aspects of these findings have been replicated with other populations of managers in various parts of the world. In recent comparative studies, Schein and her colleagues found that while female managers no longer closely associated the characteristics of good managers with male characteristics, male managers continued to do so (for example, Bremmer, Tomkiewicz and Schein 1989; Schein *et al.* 1996). These findings provide support for the possiblity of women revising their assumptions about what good management looks like to a more gender-neutral position. However, it casts doubt on the argument sometimes advanced that, as executive men become exposed to more women in the workplace, they will consciously appraise and re-evaluate their assumptions in the light of experience. I will discuss this differential receptivity to change further in Chapter 8.

That management and leadership are sex-typed constructs is confirmed by this research. It should also be acknowledged that in organisations these two constructs are often substituted. That is, if a woman is judged not to have strong management qualities, her leadership abilities will also be doubted.

Leadership is thus an attribute that observers readily associate with men. Often, it is only through a conscious act of counter-intuition that they associate it with women. The masculinity of leadership is self-perpetuating—the more men are seen to possess leadership qualities, the more status and influence they are accorded, the more they can command resources, the more formal opportunities as leaders they are offered, and the easier it is for other men to be recognised as having 'leadership potential'. This self-perpetuating loop puts great pressure on women to be like men in order to be judged as 'real leaders'.

Theory and research have not been impartial observers of the association between masculinity and leadership. One of Carol Gilligan's contributions was to show that studies of moral development, conducted either with all-male populations or without isolating gender as a variable, privileged a particular pattern of moral reasoning. The 'logic of justice', which men more than women exhibit, was simply assumed to be a higher order or more sophisticated pattern. The gender bias of models often remains obscured, while conclusions are drawn that more men exhibit the 'advanced' moral reasoning that is desirable in leadership.

The type of motivation which men more typically possess is designated in research as 'achievement motivation', while women's motivation is marginalised as driven by affiliation needs and the desire to avoid rejection. Nieva and Gutek (1981) suggest that leadership as affiliation (getting along with others to enable the job to be done) may not be a poor substitute for achievement but a different sort of leadership.

There are multiple and complex ways in which discriminatory judgements about leadership potential, or the lack of it, become deeply buried in selection processes, judgements about 'merit' (Burton 1991) and informal networks (Ibarra 1995). These structural effects are difficult for individual women managers to name and identify, let alone challenge.

A New Concept of Leadership
The Purposes of Leadership

Women's comparative invisibility in corporate leadership has, then, less to do with women than with the construct of leadership. Because leadership is always bestowed by an audience of followers or bosses, we now need to ask why it is that what women do is rarely defined as leadership.

According to Stivers the implicit equation of leadership with masculine leadership, and the resistance to changing conceptions of leadership, can only be understood by paying attention to the functions of leadership and the interests served by it:

> Our continued reliance on such a vague concept suggests that its function is ideological . . . Leadership is an important cultural myth by which we make sense of and impart significance to organizational and political experience; in addition, leadership is an idea used to support and rationalize the continuation of existing political-economic, racial and gender arrangements (1993: 59).

Prevalent images of leaders as decision-makers, visionaries and meaning-makers thus become, according to Stivers, sex-typed. In the valuing of a particular kind of vision, for example, she shows the privileging of traditional masculine concerns. This results in a continuing 'dissonance between womanhood and leadership' that is rarely held at a conscious level and therefore accessible for critique and dispute. 'In Western industrialized societies, both men and women expect leaders to be decisive, visionary, bold, and inspirational . . . they also tend to expect leaders to be male' (1993: 67).

Masculinity remains invisible and unnoticed, Stivers suggests, because stereotypical characteristics of white managerial men, such as task orientation and rationality, match the defining characteristics of managers (see also Collinson and Hearn 1996). Drawing the attention of those in the mainstream male-stream to these unconsciously held attributions and assumptions is like 'asking the fish to notice the water in which they swim' (Stivers 1996: 163). The equation of leadership with masculine leadership persists because it suits not just the interests of decision-makers who are aspiring to be leaders and tend overwhelmingly to be male, but also because leadership as masculinity resonates so deeply with wider cultural mythology: our experience of history, religion and politics; our upbringing and experience of families, schools and workplaces.

So, in order to explain why followers are ready to see leadership in certain types of men while reluctant to bestow leadership on women, we need to understand how our views towards leaders are formed and shaped by social experiences. We need to explore two ideas. The first concerns the way our earliest experiences shape later feelings towards women and towards leaders. The second idea links the learning of these earlier years to the construct of leadership as an archetype, explaining how early and old experiences endure in our adult appraisals of leaders and women.

The Origins of Our Understandings of Women and Leadership

The first relationship we have with authority and power is with mothers.* Mothers are the first leaders in our lives and the agents of our first frustrations. When asking why there are so few women leaders and seeking to understand the obstacles women face in establishing their authority, it is important to recognise the patterns of these first relationships.

Experiences in early years set the stage for life-long patterns in how we seek to win the approval and co-operation of others in powerful positions and how we console ourselves when we fail. Our feelings toward powerful men and women also have their foundations here—in our expectations of what they will, and should, do for us as followers.

Our first experience of women with authority, the mother, is one of total dependence. Later dealings with women with power can, usually unconsciously, evoke these feelings. An understanding of early relationships helps explain the often ambivalent feelings toward women with power (Bayes and Newton 1978). It also explains why greater nurturance is expected of women and why we feel greater betrayal when they behave like men. In her analysis of images of 'the monstrous feminine' in film, Creed reveals the adult terror evoked through portrayal of women's voracious sexual and reproductive urges which can occur when women are somehow out of control, rampant with power. Such a spectacle is all the more horrifying as it is the opposite of the tender nurturance that is socially decreed (Creed 1993).

---

* An earlier version of this argument appeared in the *Australian Financial Review*, 5 August 1996, p. 19.

Investigating the reasons for resistance to the ordination of women to the priesthood, Kirkman and Grieve identify a 'split in cultural images of women' between Eve and the Madonna, which they describe as 'an adult residue of a primitive emotional defence mechanism employed by the infant'. Drawing on Dinnerstein's work (1978), Kirkman and Grieve aptly describe the playing out of complex mother feelings in an unowned ambivalence about women in authority: 'two extreme attitudes towards women: . . . scapegoating them when they frustrate or threaten to be potent, or . . . idealizing them as long as they gratify' (1984: 487). It is important to note that both women and men share these ambivalent feelings about women with power.

Our adult lives contain many echoes of this infantile but Herculean struggle. One of these is the way in which our society perceives and portrays female leaders, who are often criticised because they don't nurture those below them. This criticism arises not necessarily from women's behaviour but because of our expectations. We expect women to be more sensitive to our needs and more self-denying than men. Kirkman and Grieve summarise some other outcomes in adult relationships: 'we feel more comfortable when female power is trivial and when female sexuality is controlled . . . It is more reassuring when women collude by restricting their [maternal] behaviour to a gratifying, non-judgemental and non-controlling nurturance which applauds male achievement' (1984: 488).

Similarly, subordinates can unconsciously bestow upon female authority figures the worst characteristics of their mothers— the bossiness and intrusiveness or the manipulation and pathos. Because these expectations of women and men with power are shaped at an early age, they are essentially held at an unconscious level. This means that they are resistant to inspection and hard to change.

The origins of our experiences of power also mean that women must rely on different tools and tactics to build their authority. Silence and taciturnity will often be perceived in men as evidence of restrained fatherly wisdom, but in women as quiescence, even spinelessness. Because the same behaviours are judged differentially, women need to surmount extra hurdles of expertise or commitment in order to be judged as of equivalent soundness to male colleagues.

The relationship most of us have with fathers stands in marked contrast. Typically we come to know fathers later, when our sense of self and capacity to separate is stronger. We are able to articulate feelings about fathers, to accept or reject and then get on with our lives. Fathers who work hard and are not around much are normal, taken for granted. We are much less forgiving of self-centredness in mothers; their pre-occupation with other things, not us, can be experienced as stinging rejection. When fathers are interested in our activities and supportive, we feel gratitude—when mothers do the same we don't notice because it is what we expect. And while our feelings about mothers often remain surrounded by shadowy resentments, fathers are rarely held responsible for our weaknesses and failures.

While positive memories are readily recalled, negative associations tend to be particularly deeply buried and difficult to change. This has important implications for our capacity to change our attitudes to leaders. It means that negative or ambivalent feelings about women with power are likely be particularly inaccessible. Yet at both an individual and societal level these experiences can invisibly infiltrate and distort our appraisals of women in authority when they surface in, for example, stereotyping.

Leadership as Archetype

To take into account these properties of leadership—its origins in early experiences, its often unconscious content, its construction in the interaction between leaders and their audiences—an understanding of leadership as archetype is proposed. This understanding recognises the collective and often unconscious purposes that leadership serves, helps to explain the tendency to homogeneity and 'homosexual reproduction' (Kanter 1977: 48) among leaders, and spells out the reasons for our resistance to change—why we can't readily 'see' leadership in new places.

Consistent with Jung's use of the term, archetype is defined as a powerful image or understanding which exists in the collective unconscious of groups of people. An archetype of leadership is not a style, which is a reflection of individual personality, but a social construction. It rests in the collectively experienced expectations, beliefs and feelings of a group of people, which are rarely articulated and sometimes unconscious.

While there is scope for varying interpretations about the function of archetypes, one view is that they can form a bridge between the conscious and the unconscious. As Jung notes, the content of the archetype changes once it becomes conscious; 'it takes its colour from the individual consciousness in which it happens to appear' (1968: 5). However, we can use an understanding of archetypes that may be partially revealed by behaviour, beliefs and mythology to tune into unconscious feelings.

Understanding leadership as archetype highlights the unconscious expectations and associations that we have of leaders and the collective nature of many of those associations. Thus the prevalent view that leadership will solve society's economic and social problems needs to be confronted as a powerful unconscious force, as much a product of followers' fantasies as leaders' delusions.

The concept of leadership as archetype also draws attention to many of the neglected and less well-understood dimensions of the leadership phenomenon. It explains how perceptions of who is a leader change, and it helps us to understand the dark side of leaders, the quixotic characteristics that can shade, so quickly, from charisma to demonism. Built into the leadership psyche is some degree of deviance or abnormality, and leaders are prone to particular neuroses (Lasswell, 1930; Kets de Vries, 1988; Little, 1988). Mant observes depressingly the number of inadequate leaders who 'seem to survive and flourish, spewing their neuroses all about them right to the bitter end' (1983: 5). Leaders have more certainty that 'their values deserve to serve as others' values as well', and they are not hampered by delusions of mediocrity (Hummel 1982: 210–11).

Denhardt argues that our striving for immortality, the 'most fundamental human quest' (1981: 78), underlies our attitudes to organisational leaders. Leaders inevitably become the repository for the collectively experienced fantasies of organisation members. He argues that initially, through a transference-like mechanism, organisations see salvation through the leader and many organisations support this fantasy through their ritualised hero system. Inevitably as soon as the leader acts, he or she begins to constrain, not act for, the organisation's members. Through projection, leadership then comes to represent all that is evil about an organisation, symbol of its own guilt and scapegoat. Organisations thus 'create leaders in order to destroy them' (1981: 92).

By a process of deciphering archetypes we can elucidate the mythological meanings that are often attributed to leadership. Leaders will be judged not only according to their fulfilment of the duties specified in their job description. They must also fulfil the unconscious needs of the individuals and groups in the organisation, which have been largely ignored in theories of organisation and leadership:

> Leadership is better seen as a capacity of the group, a resource which resides in the group and which must be cultivated in order for the group to fulfil its potential. Moreover, leadership must be seen as intimately connected to the process of change . . . The leader expresses not what the group is but what it might be. The leader expresses one version of the group's potential (Denhardt 1981: 130).

Leaders in the Australian business culture have traditionally had to be heroes. Organisations have recruited for the top jobs and rewarded those individual leaders who have characteristics that resonate with the history, stories and mythologies of Australian life. The people in whom we recognise heroism and leadership tend to be male and of Anglo-Celtic origin. In them are lionised attributes traditionally valued in our culture—a frontier toughness and an emotional stoicism.

Though these archetypes of corporate leadership derive from embedded cultural stories and icons, they continue to pervade the supposedly objective assessment of leadership potential in our organisations. And threaded through these archetypes are emblems of masculinity—in rites of passage, in the language of combat and sport, in jokes and assertions and demonstrations of sexual and physical prowess. Many contemporary business practices help to reproduce and perpetuate the heroic archetypes with their emphases on endurance and stoicism, on a larrikinism and light-hearted mateship, alongside a more sober paternalism.

. . .

Despite the great popularity of leadership, particularly as a subject of study in management, little attention has been given to women and leadership. This chapter has reviewed reasons for the neglect. The Absence Argument maintains that it is an inevitable outcome of the dearth of female leaders. Associated with this argument is 'the pipeline explanation'—the expectation that time and patience will remedy the absence of women and the deficiency of attention. Once more women become qualified and experienced enough to assume leadership roles in significant numbers, then they will be the subject of more significant attention. This explanation is 'woman-centred'. Women's deficiencies explain their absence from leadership, and this absence will be redressed when in sufficient numbers they, through their commitment and capabilities, earn their eligibility for leadership.

This chapter rejects the Absence Argument on several grounds. There is now an adequate pool of women with appropriate training and experience from which leaders might be selected. Further, organisations have been recruiting women for sufficient time to see them reach leadership roles. The fact that they have not indicates that the pipeline doesn't work. Indeed the pipeline is a misleading metaphor, implying that what goes in at one end eventually comes out at the other, suitably trained and groomed for leadership. The metaphor obscures the numerous invisible barriers and twists through which most men, but very few women, emerge.

The Invisibility Argument offers a more promising set of explanations for the neglect of women and leadership. This argument focuses on the construct of leadership, suggesting that masculinity is an implicit component. When women exhibit what, in a man, would be judged as leadership behaviour, they are judged as something less than, or other than, leaders. In this account, the problem lies less with women than with the way in which leadership is defined and conceptualised by followers and audiences.

This finding is the basis for us to argue for a new concept of leadership. Leadership is always a transaction, by which a group of people recognise in someone, something they have come to understand as leadership. That understanding may be strength, toughness, purpose or, more rarely, generosity and nurturance. The fundamental point is that our understandings of leadership and our recognition of who has it are embedded in broader social relations, springing from our early experiences and our socialised expectations of leaders. This concept of archetypes of leadership provides a more salient explanation for why leadership is more readily recognised in men, and in particular types of men.

About Men

3 THE TRADITIONAL PATH:
Heroic Masculinity

Being a successful corporate leader in Australia has traditionally also been an accomplishment of masculinity. Understandings of leadership and heroic masculinity have been so tightly interwoven as to be invisible and uninspected. This connection explains why, despite strong rational arguments for change, organisations remain firmly attached to traditional tests of leadership: physical stamina as the mark of commitment, emotional toughness, stoicism and self-reliance.

A significant body of international research focuses on the links between organisations and masculinities: how work defines and supports male identity, and how organisational structures and practices develop to endorse the often assumed equation between a certain way of working and the demonstration of masculinity. This research is reviewed in Chapter 4.

Yet turning to leadership research, masculinity is virtually absent as a subject of analysis. Despite men being almost universally the subject of leadership studies, masculine aspects of their leadership have been assumed or subsumed as the norm of leadership, rather than made the focus of attention. This is partially due to the continuing tendency to see both gender and sexuality as belonging to women, not men.

In contrast, I will seek to reveal in this chapter the particular masculinities inherent in traditional Australian constructions of corporate leadership, showing first historically and then by drawing on contemporary research how images of leadership and masculinity have been interwoven.

The leader's path has been one of establishing himself as a hero against culturally and mythically resonant criteria which have proved, so far, remarkably resistant to change. Despite profound changes in

cultural demographics and patterns of inter-marriage, the characteristics recognised by the workforce as leadership are heroism and
toughness, accompanied by a taciturn and rugged individualism. This
leadership is, not unexpectedly, exhibited by males of Anglo-Celtic
or European descent.* Despite the urgings of well-respected leadership gurus to move to a post-heroic leadership era, the evidence is
that most Australian organisations remain firmly wedded to the
heroic model. Why?

One reason why change has been slow is the the obscured connection between leadership and masculinities. The narrowness of
conceptions of acceptable masculinities has substantially constrained
men's and women's capacities to see and experience leadership in
new places.

Past Images of Leadership

Historians and social commentators have argued that Australia's history has shaped contemporary constructions of gender and powerful
archetypes of heroes and leaders. Robert Hughes, for example, looks
to convict society as the source of Australian mateship with its harsh
humour and unease with intimacy. The crumbling of convict society
left a powerful legacy of tough stoicism, in which survival rested on
self-reliance rather than trust.

Historian Marilyn Lake argues that it is not just history, but a
highly selective writing of history, that has shaped Australian identity
and Australian icons, in ways that exclude women. The 'independent,
free-wheeling Bushman' (Lake 1986: 122), a powerful icon of masculinity, did not recede until the early twentieth century. Though
most men were urban breadwinners from this time on, Lake shows
how the national image of the real Australian as bush hero remained
remarkably persistent and was nurtured by media portrayals of
domesticity, family and women as trampling on masculine spirit. 'A
consistent theme of our history has been the equation of masculine

---

*   In his research on multiculturalism in Australian management, Watson (1996)
      finds no obstacles at all to white South Africans being recruited into Australian
      companies. This is in marked contrast to managers who come from India,
      Pakistan and some other Asian countries.

exploits with a distinctively Australian identity—whether it be men at work in the outback or men at war overseas' (Lake 1995: 26). Judith Brett characterises the persisting contemporary version: the 'typical Australian came to be seen as a man—physically strong, resourceful, suspicious of authority, loyal to his mates, perhaps charming, but hard for a woman to catch and likely to disappoint as he bucks against the confines of domesticity' (1996: 15).

In early Australian societies women were cast in opposition to men—as whores or angels. Jill Ker Conway argues that the chronic imbalance of women and men in early settlements, and the geographical and social isolation of women, meant that these stereotypes of women remained unchallenged by experience or by women themselves. These circumstances laid the foundations of a continuing pattern in which a particular masculinity was asserted through stereotyping of women and rejection of the feminine.

In his extensive review of the construction of masculinities, Connell (1995, reminds us that particular historical settings, the social relations of settler populations, interactions with indigenous communities, the rivalry of colonising powers, and political strategies, all determine the shape and cultural form taken by dominant masculinities. Australian values of mateship, of soldier settlements, immigrant hardship and toughness in the face of outback trials, together with our wrestle with nature and preoccupation with class, are all clues to how and why the executive culture is constructed as it is. Solitary toughness in a frontier environment, facing the world from an isolated world position and not betraying weakness or vulnerability continue to shape contemporary definitions of leadership, as well as masculine success, despite contemporary rhetoric of strategic alliances and seamless global teamwork.

Writer Tim Winton laments the disabling effects of a dominant Australian masculinism on his father's generation of men: 'They were meant to be heroes, patriarchs, warriors, powerhouses, impenetrable, immovable, unyielding and without emotion' (1994: 64). Winton's observations of the burden of socialisation on ordinary men have a parallel in organisational environments: the paradox of participants actively perpetuating cultural practices about which they have profound ambivalence, but feel they have little choice. Equations of success with dominant modes of masculine interaction, as we shall see in the next chapter, extract a high price from many men. The mantle of masculinity, though striven for, can also be a prison.

Corporate Leadership

This exploration of the contemporary leadership culture draws on the *Trials at the Top* research in addition to other studies. I will conclude with brief reference to the findings of cross-cultural studies revealing how Australian workplace values differ from those in other countries.

Values, Norms and Rituals

MALENESS

Chief executives describe corporate life at the top as 'a man's world'—not just the domain of men, but

> . . . in the general sense of the culture and the team work and the way people act, it's more a male-oriented type of interaction. It can accommodate women, but it springs from a white male, older white male kind of background.

Another CEO brings a historical perspective, arguing that the impact of the war continues to be felt:

> Australia has been a man's society before the war . . . companies are still run by people who were born pre-war, during the war. Look around their Boards, their senior management is male, male, male with a capital M.

'CLUBBINESS'

Many of the *Trials at the Top* interviewees used the metaphor of the older men's club to describe the masculinism of the executive culture. There are two versions of this 'clubbiness'—an older patrician élitism and a football, locker-room larrikinism. And each has very different justifications for the exclusion of the feminine. The lure of 'cosiness' and the familiarity of shared backgrounds is described by one CEO:

. . . it's all male . . . everybody gets invited to all of the same things, you see the same people at the same social things . . . that all gets perpetuated by institutions like the Business Council . . . I've lived and worked in the United States in several cities . . . This is by far the most 'clubby', closed, senior executive environment that I've seen. I guess it all seems very comfy and very cosy . . . you wind up in a situation where it's the same people all of the time talking to each other and that doesn't promote change very well. It doesn't drive change and that's a real issue.

Another CEO focused on the schoolboy smuttiness of the second type of clubbishness:

It really is a club. It's a boys' club and they act like it's a boys' club so that manifests itself in the shady jokes, the whisperings, the jokes off to the side . . . where I have actually had to stop meetings and sit there until this group over there decides what's going on.

A third conveys the frustration he shares with other CEOs in dealing with lingering aspects of the traditional culture:

They were fed up with the sloppiness, the lack of a sense of opportunity, the lack of fairness, [the sense] that maybe some sort of old boy values will get you ahead.

The clubbiness of law firms has also been identified as an obstacle for women. When male and female lawyers were asked for descriptions of the environment at the top of large law practices, one respondent (gender unspecified) volunteered:

The three firms where I worked were treated as men's clubs from which they don't have to go home. The male partners would sit around and drink and obliquely talk about their cases and work as an excuse not to go home. It was perceived as a threat that you had a life outside the firm.

These practices were described as hours of 'worship' rather than work by a male respondent in the same survey (Liverani 1995: 36).

SOLIDARITY

That traditional Australian value of mateship takes distinctive forms in the corporate environment. Despite an emphasis on individualism and sturdy self-reliance, historically Australian employees have also showed a solidarity and a commitment to fight for collective rights which is not characteristic of other nations such as the United States. This is sometimes associated, as popularly noted, with the Tall Poppy Syndrome—an appetite for attacking or undermining high achievers, bringing them down to the level of the rest. Traditionally (though this may be changing), our most admired sporting heroes are not those who boast or exhibit temperamental stardom. We have honoured those who wear their achievements lightly and attribute them to hard work and dedication rather than brillance.

The kind of togetherness and mateship we see at senior levels is certainly not the admiration for ambition seen in some American organisations, or the emotional openness and declarations of vulnerability which women use as the benchmark of friendship. Rather it is a shoulder-to-shoulder solidarity which unites against adversity and does the right thing by included others—those who are mates. The adversity that unites might be a business competitor or a predator, but it can also be women or, more generally, perceived feminine values of weakness. In this case, solidarity takes the form of a determined heterosexuality which has women in their place (in support roles in organisation and at home) and order in the world.

This solidarity can, of course, become imprisoning, and allow little deviance. Inclusiveness is defined by exclusion—frequently of women, gay men or men of different cultural and racial backgrounds. This particular interpretation of solidarity also helps to explain the slow pace of reform in the Australian union movement. Despite the efforts of capable female leaders, including Jenni George, the current ACTU President, union hierarchies have been resistant to recognising the rising proportion of female members and adjusting their practices and processes to be inclusive of women.

Many Australian organisations espouse commitment to 'a people-oriented culture', extolling the importance of more feminine values such as caring and helping employees to be their best. Yet the reality is often very different. There is tacit agreement in leadership ranks that, although in principle people are important, in practice tougher tactics are frequently necessary.

SPORT AND SPORTING HEROES

Studies of masculinities and male-dominated cultures frequently identify a common interest in sport as a test of acceptable masculinity. In her work on the European Union, Woodward (1996) found that football was the language and interest which crossed otherwise quite significant cultural differences between European bureaucrats. Connell (1995) encourages us to understand a common interest in sport among men as historically constructed, persisting because it serves political purposes—of including some while excluding others (men and women) and of reproducing hierarchies, especially as sport increasingly becomes big business.

Sporting heroes are compelling objects of identification. For men in particular, though not exclusively, the illusion that such heroes are supernaturally strong, courageous and physically gifted offers moments of mythical resonance—when human frailty can be overcome and one can identify with a grander order of achievement.

In the contemporary construction of executive culture these values are reinforced in rituals: attending football or cricket; doing business over a game of tennis or squash, or in the exclusive atmosphere of the golf club or 'corporate box'. Maleness and executive eligibility are simultaneously demonstrated through these processes, and in turn defined by the absence, if not exclusion, of women.

LEADERSHIP AS COMBAT

Much of the language and metaphor of the executive culture is either militaristic or derives from male contact sports. Physical combat is a predominant image in executive exchanges and pain is publicly inflicted. Conflict in meetings is described as 'taking body blows'. In her study of thirteen public-sector chiefs, Saunders found the battleground, and the inevitability of suffering and inflicting pain, a common metaphor for the task of leading organisations:

> I do a lot of talking to the troops. There hasn't been too much blood lost. People need to be prepared to put in the pain.

I look for middle managers who are keen and hungry and will suffer the pain . . . those who are prepared to engage in activities that might cost them pain.

CEOs talk of the inevitability of 'a lot of fighting in the trenches', and that sometimes 'you're better off just burying your dead and working around them'. Cultural change is 'largely a process of pushing and shoving' requiring the use of 'some pretty blunt instruments' (Saunders 1996).

Attributes of the Leader

This account of the environment of corporate leaders renders it less than inviting. However, the scale of obstacles and toughness create all the more opportunities for a particular form of heroism to be exhibited. Leaders have a vested interest in glorifying the battle, since it enhances their own triumph in surviving and succeeding. One CEO put it this way:

The higher up you go, the more an act of courage is required . . . It is a very courageous act to take on a top job because it's an immense responsibility and it is something which places a fear, a great physical and emotional load on you if you are going to lead properly . . . [Aspiring women leaders are judged] a bit different. It's an extra load and, I suspect, quite a significant load for a woman. In other words, their ambition does not extend to really going to the absolute top. (Saunders 1996)

In this eloquent statement, leadership is defined via the acts of courage demanded and the fears and load withstood. It is also defined by the presence of something women don't have.

Several values at the core of the Australian leadership culture can be identified. This list, which is not exhaustive or final, emerges from my *Trials at the Top* research, as well as from other work cited in this chapter:

- heroism (rejecting weakness, valuing displays of courage);
- physical toughness (exhibiting stamina and endurance, experienced at working in difficult physical conditions);
- emotional toughness (phlegmatic, not showing weakness, not flinching or recoiling from what needs to be done);

- self-reliance (exhibiting drive, not dependent on or vulnerable to others).

Corporate rituals and practices, both inside and outside the organisation, support and advance these values in a whole range of ways. Inside the organisation, leaders:

- work extraordinarily long hours, regularly working weekends and attending evening work functions;
- rarely take sick leave and often have accrued annual leave;
- see sacrifice of personal and family time as necessary for the job;
- demand and demonstrate a capacity to travel at short notice and be available for overseas work.

Most large organisations carry significant leave liabilities due to a continued reluctance of managers to take accrued annual leave. Despite espoused company policy, the embedded habit is that senior managers don't take leave. It is interesting to speculate on why this is so and why many organisations have been forced to take drastic measures to force executives to take their leave—some of whom eventually do so, but turn up to work anyway. An explanation for this reluctance often put forward is fear that in their absence managers may be superseded or found redundant. While the actual incidence of managers losing jobs while on leave is not high, that such fears are pervasive is further evidence of the relentless pressure imposed by the heroic culture.

One could, alternatively, ask why senior managers find the prospect of spending time at home or with family so terrifying. Perhaps their status in the private domain is more fragile and often challenged. Less flippantly, it seems likely that when men work Herculean schedules, they are not just accomplishing the organisation's task, but are engaged in other emotional work as well. Identities are being nourished, power and self-importance validated. And they may not be working excessively, despite long hours at the office (Hochschild 1997). In part, these men feel better being at work than at home—they feel indispensable and powerful—and a sense of purpose is being earned. Conforming to a model of heroic leadership also delivers benefits for masculinity. Conversely, not embracing these behaviours leaves leaders open to being seen as 'not tough enough' or 'not committed enough' to join the ranks of the heroic warriors. The men who eschew this pattern face a double burden of defending their alternative paths while simultaneously demonstrating their credentials as men.

Outside organisational hours, leaders exhibit:

- an interest, ideally a background or demonstrated prowess and readiness to be involved in sport, particularly football, cricket, tennis and golf, as well as yachting, cycling, horse-racing, basketball and so on;
- a capacity to be available for, and participate in, social rituals, in turn often centred around sport.

The reproduction of these values and norms, in the Australian context, often entails:

- the rejection of so-called feminine traits such as patience, nurturance, weakness or need for protection;
- the rejection of other men who do not conform to the norms and rituals, for example gay men, men who eschew sporting interests, those who work at home, work part-time or are looking after children;
- the rejection of 'quality of life' or concerns of balance.

Cross-cultural Perspectives

In international comparisons, Australians value individualism and masculinity, and are not as comfortable with hierarchy as some other, particularly Asian, societies (Hofstede 1980; Gibson 1995). This translates into a leadership style which emphasises self-reliance and independence.

Australians also put a higher value on leisure and quality of life than many of the countries against which we habitually compare ourselves (Super 1995). These values are expressed and institutionalised through a preoccupation with sport and with social activities organised around watching sport. Australians like to think of themselves as an easy-going and athletic nation, and habits of combining business with sport (on the golf course, at the tennis or football), preserve these values.

While both Australia and the United States score highly on individualism and masculinity, these emphases take different forms when looking at leaders. Australian employees place greater emphasis on extrinsic factors such as job security and income (Dowling and Nagel 1986), expecting their leaders to be directive, even autocratic (Gibson 1995). At the same time, they are inclined to be sceptical of leadership. Whereas American leaders receive the respect of employees until they demonstrate themselves unworthy, Australian employees 'start with a negative attitude towards their leaders until they prove they are deserving of respect' (Parry, reported in James 1996).

Many large Australian companies share a global expansion strategy. From banking to brewing, resource extraction to manufacturing, companies are seeking to expand their operations into various parts of the world, but particularly into the Asian and South-East Asian region. As already noted, Australia is among the most multicultural societies in the world, yet corporate leadership remains homogeneously Anglo-Celtic. A study by Egon Zehnder of twenty-five Australian companies with at least 10 per cent of assets offshore found that of 255 directors (200 non-executive directors), 93 per cent are domiciled in Australia. There are only 8 foreign resident directors, 3 on one company Board. The authors cite one board chairman expressing an explicit preference for Melbourne-resident directors and they conclude: 'in geographic terms . . . diversity at Board level is a non issue'.

Turning to the track records and priorities of senior managers, Hunt (1995) found that among fifty-four senior Australian executives, international experience was ranked last of twenty-three items in their own management development. 'International experience' was thus assessed as less relevant to their success as leaders than, for example, 'an eye for detail'. Similarly, research for the Industry Taskforce on Leadership and Management (1995) by Boston Consulting Group contrasted the executive profile of the 1970s, 1990s and 2010. The executives of 1970 and today are both male, of Anglo-Celtic origin, with much of their career spent in one organisation— a product of internal management training. They describe a transition from a 'very local' to 'expanding focus', with overseas travel more common in the 1990s.

The Industry Taskforce report contrasted this profile with the leader/enabler of 2010, who is male or female, comes from a wide range of cultural backgrounds, and not only travels overseas but has lived and managed workforces in several countries. While the Taskforce sees sophisticated people-skills and greater comfort with diversity as essential to continued economic growth, the report notes incontrovertible evidence of slowness in training and developing these skills.

Looking to existing leadership to initiate such change may, for reasons elaborated below, be overly hopeful. Discussing the link between cross-cultural experiences and organisational change, Menadue (1996) argues that the Board and chief executive levels are where most resistance to change occurs. Those who have successfully ascended to such levels are 'reluctant to admit that the system needs changing' and are typically insulated from the intense, paradigm-changing experiences that often result from doing business on the ground in other cultures. Visiting an overseas subsidiary is one thing; having to run an effective operation in such a location is quite another.

Why Heroic Leadership Persists

Societies continue to look for leadership and individuals aspire to becoming leaders. In Chapter 2 I suggested that one of the reasons for our attachment to particular images of leadership lies in our earliest experiences—interactions with fathers and mothers, as well as early experiences with institutions and social structures.

Two other sets of reasons help to explain why existing and aspiring leaders continue to idealise (often unconsciously) and benefit from, notions of heroic leadership. The first set has to do with what heroism offers—a chance to be great, to be revered, perhaps even to glimpse immortality. The second, more pragmatic, set is linked to the first but looks at the strong interest that leaders and aspiring leaders have in preserving the arduousness of the journey to the top and the exclusivity once one is there.

In *Trials at the Top* I compared the leadership quest of the contemporary executive to the journey Odysseus makes in Greek and Roman mythology. Odysseus (also called Ulysses) spends ten years returning to home and his patient wife Penelope after the sacking of Troy. Among many perils, he endures nine life-threatening disasters, each of which is said to be a metaphor for death. These trials involve battling with a one-eyed giant as well as withstanding temptations. The temptations typically are presented by voracious women, who attempt to seduce Odysseus into giving up or succumbing to earthly weaknesses. There are also loving and trusting women who support Odysseus and bear him children. However, the moral is that, ultimately, he must not be diverted, even by genuine love.

It is through enduring the trials and withstanding weakness and temptation that Odysseus proves himself. Surviving trials and pain are also, of course, a central part of the initiation ceremonies among traditional societies. Initiation ceremonies take more sadistic and sinister forms in military and all-male colleges (see Cameron 1997). Evidence of the regulation of rites of passage by groups of men to establish the eligibility and inclusion of other men is well-documented in anthropological and sociological literature.

Trials in the executive's journey, like these initiations, function to differentiate potential leaders from the rest. The unsuccessful are those who seek respite: 'They can't manage a second period of change. They think that having done it once, that's enough'.

> Sometimes their motivation just stops, eases back . . . We get a lot of people like this. Sometimes they get married, and their value systems change; sometimes they fall in love with a particular location and don't want to move somewhere else; sometimes they have some trauma in their family that causes them to not want to devote the time or the effort to what they are doing; sometimes they reach a standard of living, a standard of comfort, that satisfies them and they are not motivated to go further—a whole variety of personal factors. Sometimes they lose the will to continue to learn.

In this scenario there is no triumph, and no leadership, without adversity. In Australian organisations, this adversity and one's capacity to triumph above it, are cast in ways which are distinctly masculine, but also value certain sorts of masculine performances: 'The successful executive is able to go from crisis to crisis and manage them effectively, keep doing it. They've got to do it all their career'. They are permitted to make mistakes, but executive eligibility is demonstrated in the expectation that the tough times will keep on coming; executive success in insatiably facing up to crises without being destroyed by them.

The heroic archetype of leadership is a construction in which leaders have much at stake. Good executives are portrayed as superhuman and larger than life: 'bigger than themselves', 'the best in the world', 'the men at the top'. They must be the sum of many, more mediocre, men: 'the executive has to be the collection of talent in himself or herself'. Executives stride a global stage: 'They have to be part of the world and not just part of Australia'; and 'in this world you have to be a little better than the locals'. Leaders must demonstrate a capacity to rise above their technical or functional core to achieve a transcendent wisdom; having 'the ability to sit on top and understand the connections between things'. Only the most courageous and capable succeed: 'Those that make it are very good'. To be judged a leader among this league of heroes is a prize indeed.

This construction of heroic leadership explains why Australian leaders have so little real interest in change. Leading men have a stake in their jobs being understood as barely do-able, in the demands being relentless and themselves irreplaceable, because they are the only ones who can stay on top of the job. This construction of leadership also explains why there is contempt in managerial quarters when the possibility of part-time work or job-sharing is raised. When such innovations are ventured, the retort is incredulous: 'You couldn't do this job part-time!' And for companies that have arrangements for flexible working hours, the take-up among managerial men is almost non-existent.

Rarely is the ideal of heroic leadership questioned in corporate circles. Among those leaders who do advocate and work for a different kind of leadership, personal and family experiences have often forced them to question the price which the heroic path can exact (see Chapter 4). Frequently, those who remain committed to the ideal regard them suspiciously, as failed or fallen.

Leadership ideology serves the purpose of perpetuating particular social and economic practices. It is important to recognise that, when backed by a culturally embedded but formally unrecognised ideology of masculinity, the combination is powerful, perhaps unmoveable. The unspoken intertwining of ideologies of leadership and masculinity serve the important purposes of maintaining the status quo, the privilege of an élite, and of perpetuating assumed assessments of who looks like 'leadership material'.

Achieving masculinity while doing leadership accrues extra sources of power for men. These sources of power are stronger for their invisibility. Audiences may simply feel more reassured by the paternal and masterly performance of a strong male leader. Leaders look like fathers, not like mothers. As well as serving these purposes, there is a psychological pay-off for some men in proving leadership through a rejection of the feminine.

For all these reasons, existing leaders are unlikely to advocate radical changes in leadership. Asked for their visions of change, institutional leaders will typically volunteer incremental change dressed in the rhetoric of globalism and borderlessness. They forsee change for others, but less for themselves.

John Kotter (1990), one of management's most adulated gurus on leadership, distinguishes leaders from managers precisely on the basis of their capacity to envisage change and transform organisations. Yet corporate Australia has a history of selecting and training its leaders from within. Although there are exceptions to this convention, when outsiders and particularly Americans are recruited to lead Australian organisations, such radical moves are generally reserved for extreme situations. And it is revealing that it often takes an outsider to execute a dramatic turnover of leadership when an organisation is on the verge of self-destruction.

· · ·

Despite substantial bodies of organisational and feminist research, the leadership literature remains largely silent on leadership's relationship to masculinity and sexuality. The study of leadership, from Weber to contemporary gurus, 'excludes women and fails to problematize men and masculinity in relation to leadership' (Collinson and Hearn 1994: 4). It is worth noting that this exclusion is particularly marked in the management and organisational psychology literature which is rapidly digested by management training organisations around the world (see Sinclair 1995a, 1995d). The closest that much of this research gets are studies which demonstrate consistent association of the constructs of 'masculine' and 'leadership', while not problematising this association. A more modest research endeavour, described in detail in the next chapter, examines the association between management, leadership and masculinities. With some exceptions, it comes out of a critical European tradition and has been far less influential in managerial curricula and thinking than the vast bulwark of leadership theory.

A number of authors, Charles Handy (1989) among them, argue that a sea-change is occurring in organisational leadership, from the heroic to the 'post heroic'. While the heroic leader achieves by his own Herculean efforts—knowing all and doing all—the post-heroic leader seeks to solve problems and achieve outcomes through developing the capabilities of others.

Handy's emphasis on a more people-oriented leadership, one in which leaders have the capacity to set aside ego, or at least achieve ego gratification through more indirect means, echoes the earlier predictions, or hopes, of scholars of leadership. For example, Burns distinguished transactional leaders, who lead by initiating transactions and exchange of valued things, from transformational leaders, who lead by building relationships. These relationships are characterised by conditions 'of mutual stimulation and elevation that converts followers into leaders and may convert leaders into moral agents' (Burns 1978).

Despite these predictions, and the often-recited 'human capital' arguments which warn against overlooking the talents of those with different backgrounds and experience (see Chapter 8), the Australian corporate environment continues to define leadership in heroic terms. Heroism takes on particular characteristics of stoicism, self-reliance, emotional and physical toughness and stamina which derive from the peculiar historical and cultural conditions of Australia's origins. The values of the leadership culture do not simply equate with notional 'universal' masculinity. Historical and cultural forces have forged the particular links we now document between corporate leadership and heroic masculinity in the Australian context.

There is undoubtedly some disquiet about the 'downsides' of this heroic archetype. On the one hand, men relish the sense of achievement in surviving and succeeding in such a tough environment. And it has the comfort of familiarity. On the other, there seems to be a desire to grow up from it or beyond it. There is discontent about the way the culture works, supported by increasing unease about the valuable and potentially advantageous perspectives it excludes.

Despite these reservations, the heroic archetype has proved remarkably resistant to change. And its persistence should not surprise us. Aspiring leaders as well as those who are already recognised as leaders have an interest in preserving this construction. It is supported by society's attachment to cultural myths and icons, and it is in turn supported by a political and economic ideology of business élitism.

But more significantly, another stake which society has in the heroic leader construction has to do with traditional gender relations and with supporting the implicit equation of masculinity and leadership. Unwritten but central to Australian corporate leadership has been its masculine character. Proving oneself as a leader has also served to prove oneself as a man. Building a career is also a process of constructing an admired masculine identity. Becoming a leader is not just a career landmark but proof of one's maleness. Until we expose the nexus between these two constructs, we cannot fully understand the basis for resistance to change in leadership and how new constructs of leadership might emerge.

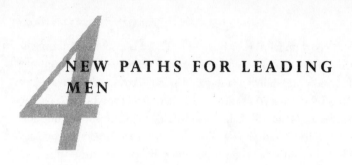

NEW PATHS FOR LEADING MEN

There are compelling reasons for men to question prevalent masculinities—but are they? Findings from our interviews and elsewhere indicate such a questioning among some managers and leaders. At the same time we note the reasons why most men remain unwilling or unable to do so. The evidence is that the catalysts for questioning typically comes from circumstances outside men's control, or from negotiations with wives and children that are often forced upon them rather than initiated by men.

Masculinity and Men in Organisations

Masculinity refers to gender identity as a man, a historically and socially constructed category which defines what are deemed appropriate behaviours and identities for men. Although, for some men, their sense of masculinity may be tied to their physiology and sex, or their sexual preference, it is important, for reasons elaborated below, to differentiate these nominations from masculinity.

Traditionally, for most men, their sense of masculinity or of themselves as men has been unnoticed, unexamined and unquestioned. Masculinity has been so assumed, so normal, so woven into the fabric of history, of events, of public life, that it has not needed a label. Reinforced by social norms which rewarded its expression—the protective breadwinner, the strong athlete, the good mate, the capable mechanic, the man of the world, the powerful leader—the fact that these were also men, and expressions of masculinity, escaped notice.

Why are we talking about masculinities now? In his comprehensive overview of the analysis of masculinity, Bob Connell (1995) notes that several strands of theory and science coming together in the late twentieth century have focused our attention on masculinities: anthropology and ethnographies, history and sociology, psycho-analysis and feminism. I want to focus on three more contemporary influences, encompassing research and popular movements. These are feminism, the men's movement, and gay and lesbian scholarship and popular culture (see also Collinson and Hearn 1994).

Feminism must, to some extent, take credit for encouraging us to systematically examine the effects of gender, to go past the obser-vation that a man is a man and a woman is a woman and to record the structural ways in which gender systematically frames experience and opportunities. Feminist historians, for example, helped us to see that the assumption of male heroes not only obscured the contri-bution of women but systematically reproduced the mythology that history was made by men. And feminism has prompted a revisiting of the early psychological research on sex-roles which vastly overstated the biological basis of the differences between men and women.

For some time, gender analyses were designed to show how women had been excluded and how femininity had been devalued and marginalised beenss a huge range of fields—from medical research to historical accounts, from politics to literature. Efforts to give women's experience and achievements greater voice and power were central to this agenda.

In directing attention to gender, feminism has thus been central. At the same time, it has been women's gender, the deviant from the norm, that has been the focus. For example, until the 1980s the vast majority of books purporting to be about gender—by both female and male authors—are actually about women (see, for example, Illich 1982). This helps to perpetuate the assumption that only women have gender and it happens to be the troublesome one.

Although many justifiably argue that the new focus on women corrected a long-overdue neglect, an unintended by-product has been the institutionalisation of theories of what Eveline calls 'women's disadvantage' (1994; 1996). When we think of gender, we think of women. Women come to signify the theory and the problems of gender. Eveline argues for a shift away from assessing 'women's disadvantage', instead focusing on 'the politics of advantage'— the way maleness systematically accrues invisible advantage. To some degree, recent attention to masculinities begins to redress the equation of gender and women. It recognises that men have gender and that gender is not simply biological but is a social and political construction which in turn has extensive social and economic ramifications, for men as well as women.

The American-based Men's Movement of the 1970s and 1980s gathered momentum with popular publications like Warren Farrell's *The Liberated Man* (1974) and quite a bit later Robert Bly's *Iron John: A Book about Men* (1990). Much of this work was a barely veiled reaction against feminism. In simplified terms, the way to rediscover and reassert manliness, according to this prescription, was to resuscitate old icons and habits of men. Men should re-find their warrior roots and celebrate all that is different to women. Resulting popular prescriptions for a resuscitated masculinity rested on over-reactions to 'femininity' (as perceived) and the belief that in order to establish masculinity women should be subordinated.

As Connell (1995) points out, these popular directions had been foreshadowed much earlier in psychoanalysis. In 1932 Karen Horney published a paper in the *International Journal of Psychoanalysis* entitled 'The Dread of Women'. Although subsequently neglected by mainstream psychoanalysis, these ideas have been more recently revived in discussions of 'fear of the feminine', an argument analysed in more detail in Chapter 8.

Increasing attention to sexualities has also been a catalyst for attention to masculinities. The view widely and powerfully argued by gay communities that men, and women, who are predominantly homosexual, are no less men or women, has prompted a decoupling of gender identity from sexual identity. In turn, this has provoked rethinking of what it is to be a man. Defining a man through his heterosexuality was clearly revealed to be inadequate, just as defining a man through his simple biological difference to women was revealed to be hopelessly insufficient.

Through the process of examining sexualities it emerged that indeed, in the eyes of society, all men are not equal. Some men are seen to be 'more manly' than others: 'experience of masculinity and of being a man are not uniform' (Hearn and Morgan 1990: 11). The concept of 'hegemonic masculinity' has been extended and developed by theorists such as Connell (1987) and Hearn to underline that certain forms and practices of masculinity are dominant under particular socio-cultural and economic régimes. Simultaneously, other practices of masculinity will co-exist but not be privileged. 'This implies that men too, within a society that may be characterized as "patriarchal", may experience subordinations, stigmatizations or marginalizations as a consequence of their sexuality, ethnic identity, class position, religion or marital status' (Hearn and Morgan 1990: 11). Connell draws on case and profile data to explore the construction of several marginal masculinities in Australia: young, unemployed men; new age, environmental, activist men; and homosexual men also employed in 'straight' occupations.

Masculinities are thus multiple, with varying power, and historically and culturally they are continually being remade (Tacey 1997). In this remaking, power is central, with the result that a dominant interpretation of masculinity is enacted and reproduced by an élite, which also represses alternative masculinities.

The concept of hegemonic masculinity goes a long way towards explaining why men with power resist examining or questioning their own maleness. There are arguments both about perception and about power here. Firstly, hegemonic masculinity may be so taken for granted and assumed that it is unobservable to men. This is the reason why it will often be women who are more able, and willing, to identify maleness or masculinity as a phenomenon for discussion. For men, its existence is so assumed that it is imperceptible and therefore beyond debate.

Secondly though, and this is the power argument, hegemonic masculinity serves the purposes and interests of powerful men. Through it, their particular enactment and expression of male leadership, of largely heterosexual masculine dominance, remains uncontested and admired, by other men and by women.

The Costs of Hegemonic Masculinity

Traditional and narrow constructions of acceptable masculinities, it is argued, have become a prison for some men. Across many fields there is increasing attention given to analysing how these constructions fail young men at school and in early adulthood, and older men in caring for their health. Although clearly, broader economic and social factors, in particular chronic unemployment and economic disadvantage, offer part of the explanation, it is still instructive to analyse the attitudes and behaviours these studies find in men at risk. The findings have some consistency. Studies of boys' school performance, of risk-taking in young male drivers, of the suicides of young adults who are overwhelmingly male, of men suffering from various stress-related illnesses, all document a recognisable pattern of behaviours and attitudes. There is a stance of professed invincibility (often masking lack of connection), a pattern of risk-taking, a failure to take seriously signs of illness, a difficulty seeking help or advice, an apparent inability to express emotions and to discharge, in a comparatively safe way, anxieties and fears.

It is not hard to see the features of heroic masculinity identified in the preceding chapter—heroism, physical and emotional toughness and self-reliance—in another instance and context go terribly wrong. Those working with young men lament, in particular, the demise of culturally sanctioned and safe processes in which old identities as boys can be dissolved and young men can test themselves physically and spiritually before earning membership of the broader tribe of men (for example, Tacey 1995).

A vast array of statistics assembled by psychologist Gail Sheehy (1994) attests to the costs of what she describes as the Samson Syndrome, a tendency among men to define themselves in terms of their work and their sexual potency. Although behind these statistics lie complex issues of causation and measurement, at a gross level they reveal traditional expressions of maleness as a significant risk factor to the health and safety of men. These are some of the findings:

- At the turn of the century women and men tended to die at around the same age (between 47 and 49). Now men die on average six years earlier than women.
- Men have a higher rate of depression than women and are at four times greater risk of suicide. The leading cause of death among men aged between 12 and 60 is self-inflicted death.
- Almost as many men die of prostate cancer as women die of breast cancer, yet the amount of research and resources devoted to prevention and cure don't compare.

And, according to the Victorian Health Promotion Foundation

- Men 'routinely fail at close relationships' (four out of five divorces are initiated by women).
- Over 90 per cent of convicted acts of violence will be carried out by men and 70 per cent of the victims will be men.
- In school, 90 per cent of children with behaviour problems will be boys and over 80 per cent of children with learning difficulties will be boys.*

In the popular literature, several sets of contemporary costs of traditional hegemonic masculinity have similarly been identified:

MASCULINITY AS A HEALTH HAZARD

Because of men's traditional reliance on women to look after them, men fare badly on a range of health indicators, particularly after marriage break-ups. Women's biology (for example, menstruation and pregnancy) encourages them to take note of their bodies and physiology. In contrast, men's biology means they will often not seek medical advice until much later in life, and men's upbringing encourages them to ignore sickness and endure pain. In sports these qualities are lionised. Boys learn to hide their emotions very early and by adulthood many men are afflicted by alexithymia or emotional numbness (Levant 1995). Denial of emotion, combined with risk-taking and aggressiveness, means that men are slow to seek medical attention and so contributes to their lower life expectancy.

ATTENUATED FAMILY RELATIONSHIPS

Having a family and children of which one can be proud is an important badge of manliness, but numbers of men express regret and a sense of impotence about lost or stunted relationships with children. One executive in *Trials at the Top* talked of the floating resentment: '"What's a bloke doing driving his kids home from school?" Nobody says that's wrong but there's still something of that going around'. There is evidence of men seeking to have closer relationships with their children than their fathers had with them (Smith 1995), although there are ambivalent feelings about whether and how to

* Victorian Health Promotion Foundation Symposium pamphlet advertising 'Challenges and change for men in the 21st century and the women they work and live with', 7 May 1997, Melbourne.

invest the emotional labour necessary to create and sustain better family relationships (Mulholland 1996).

A SHAKY SENSE OF MALENESS AND OVERREACTION TO FEMINISM

Novelist Tim Winton sees men under huge pressure to do, to build and create, to act and do great deeds. And playwright Tony Ayres says, 'masculinity is a much shakier identity than femininity . . . [boys] must do things to find an identity where girls can just be' (*Age* Green Guide, 29 Feb. 1996). Ayres also warns that because men are not accustomed to verbalising what they do, there is a danger that it will be seen as an inferior version of what women do—for example, that men's grief or men's friendship is somehow lesser because it is talked about less.

Fears about the future of men were summarised in a widely reproduced article from the *Economist* with the heading 'Men: Are They Necessary' (*Australian*, 30 Dec. 1995). It not only itemised the physical frailty of the male species, but showed how technology might render them reproductively irrelevant.

Some of the popular debate has descended to scare tactics, failing to distinguish men from masculinities and attacking feminism. However flawed though, this discussion has focused attention on a pattern of behaviours and attitudes, ways of living and working, that were previously unproblematised. It has also provided a forum for many men, who had been struggling with what society seemed to require of them, to voice their discontent and dissent.

Managerial Masculinities

Early work on managerial masculinity portrayed a privileged masculinity placing and enforcing unquestioned values of instrumentalism, control, rationality, and either technical knowledge or hierarchy as the basis of authority. Subsequent research has illuminated the dynamism in constructions of managerial masculinities.

In their exploration of management cultures, researchers have now begun to document the variety of masculinities which are expressed and enacted in organisational environments. Following her early work on the masculine cultures of shopfloor workers (1983; 1985), Cynthia Cockburn investigated British retail organisations, expanding her analysis to managerial levels (1991). Also in Britain, Collinson (1992), Maddock and Parkin (1993), Parkin and Maddock (1995), Roper (1991, 1994) and Collinson and Hearn (1994), among others, have documented how managerial subcultures are built around masculinities. Collinson and Hearn (1994), for example, have itemised the following varieties:

- traditional authoritarianism (advanced through bullying and fear);
- gentleman's club (protective paternalism accompanied by born to rule);
- entrepreneurialism (task focused, workaholism; see also Mulholland 1996);
- informalism (boyish, larrikin-like culture, attached to ritualism of sports and sex);
- careerist (valuing expertise and bureaucratic advancement).

Maddock and Parkin (1993) point out that each masculine culture or subculture has different vehicles and rationalisations for women's ineligibilities for management. In the case of 'the gentleman's club', there is an ethos of kindly over-protection from which some women initially benefit and collude. The 'barrack yard' culture of police, fire protection and military services, which is built on extreme needs for discipline in emergency situations, often culminates in chronic bullying in everyday management style. The 'locker room' privileges male heterosexuality, sexualising women in organisations. Maddock and Parkin identify three more recent masculine cultures in which the subjugation of women is less explicit and consequently more difficult to tackle. In the 'gender blind culture' management treats everyone as if they were men, justifying this sameness as evidence of equality. Similarly, the 'feminist pretenders' culture sounds well-versed in principles of equality, but creates new stereotypes and new forms of oppression by expecting all women to act as change agents. Finally, the 'smart macho' culture is 'driven by extreme competitivity; [managers] discriminate against those who cannot work at the same pace or who challenge the economic criteria' (1995: 76).

'Smart macho' cultures are perhaps the most difficult, but important, to challenge. While they do not discriminate against women *per se*, they are increasingly the experience of corporate life. What happens in such cultures is that the definition of managerial work and success becomes inextricably linked to demonstrated behaviours such as working very long hours and exhibiting high levels of aggressiveness and competitiveness. While not impossible for women to meet these criteria, it is more difficult, requiring a higher level of personal sacrifice and greater emotional toughness—since women exhibiting the same aggressiveness, for example, are judged less approvingly by peers and bosses.

In the United States, early research on masculinities tended to focus more on the popular Men's Movement and rather less on institutional masculinities. However, Kimmel lists the 'rules of masculinity' which Brannon, in his study of American men in the early 1970s, found readily apparent in the leadership cultures of organisations:

- No sissy stuff: avoid all behaviours that even remotely suggest the feminine.
- Be a big wheel: success, status and superiority confer masculinity.
- Be a sturdy oak: reliability and dependability are defined as emotional and affective distance.
- Give 'em hell: exude an aura of manly aggression, go for it, take risks (Kimmel 1990).

The extent to which these 'rules' are constructed on rejection of characteristics associated with women, such as vulnerability and connection, is noted by Maupin and Lehman (1994). Kimmel argues that while this expression of masculinity is not biologically determined, it is the standard against which other masculinities are compared. 'It is a masculinity that is always willing to take risks, able to experience pain and not submit to it, driven constantly to accumulate (power, money, sexual partners)' (1990: 100).

Meanwhile, in psychological research, leadership had come to be associated with masculinity. Psychological measures and tests, for example the Bem Sex Role Inventory (1974), have both recorded and institutionalised the association between leadership and masculinity. The BSRI was developed by asking people to rate the desirability of a list of characteristics for a man or a woman. The resulting inventory contains twenty items which were rated significantly more desirable in a man, twenty items rated more desirable in a woman and twenty judged as neutral or equally desirable. The masculine items include 'acts as a leader' and 'has leadership abilities' while the feminine items include 'childlike', 'shy' and 'yielding'. The BSRI undoubtedly records recognisable stereotypes. However, its continued and sometimes unproblematised use contributes to the perpetuation of those stereotypes—that leadership requires particular masculine behaviours and feminine characteristics are opposed to leadership.

In her research on American men in the 1990s, Gail Sheehy finds men in middle-age and late middle-age firmly wedded to work and sexual performance as the main means to measure themselves as men. This is despite the statistical evidence that many men in middle-age are looking to long lives ahead with neither high-status careers nor high levels of sexual potency to assure their status as men.

Studies of workplaces have thus increasingly revealed how masculinity is interwoven into the cultural and institutional presumptions of organisation and managerial leadership, while organisation is reinforced by particular masculine practices and expression. While the focus of early work was on blue-collar environments, which are comparatively low-status workplaces, recent work reveals the adaption and re-making of masculinities in the new corporate order and in very senior levels of organisations.

Conducting a study of the British financial services industry, Kerfoot and Knights (1993) identified how traditional paternalism, a long-standing hallmark of organisational masculinity, was giving way to a competitive masculinity. Part of this shift was attributable to a new philosophy of strategic management and, particularly, to the imperative for growth. Paternal masculinity had, they argued, been built on a nineteenth-century conception of gentlemanly behaviour, sustained by social privilege, a belief in the 'natural right to govern' and a gender order in which women need to be protected. Competitive masculinity defines work as a rational and depersonalised enterprise, although a 'synthetic sociability' and 'purposive intimacy' are fostered via team building and other human resource management initiatives. The place of sexuality in the two masculinities is thus very different:

> . . . in contrast to bureaucracy, where sexual relations contradict the demands of the impersonal, rule-based order, strategic management seeks to channel energies that might be 'dissipated' in sexual encounters into activities designed to accomplish organizational objectives. But while bureaucracy segregates sex, emotion and 'the personal' from the functionary, displacing it onto the 'private' sphere, strategic management could be said to utilize sexuality in its operation (Kerfoot and Knights 1993: 670).

In competitive masculinity, others—from competitors to subordinates—become objects of control: 'caught in ceaseless striving for material and symbolic success . . . conquest and domination become exalted as ways of relating to the world'. The drive to control inevitably also extends to self, creating a precarious masculinity which requires constant confirmation in a world which 'presents itself as a never-ending series of challenges and conquests' (Kerfoot and Knights 1993: 672).

In their longitudinal study of 461 auditors, Maupin and Lehman found that being successful in accounting organisations involved 'suppressing or eliminating attitudes and behaviours that would identify them as "typically female"'. Every partner, both men and women, exhibited high masculinity scores, and those with the highest scores were more likely to have higher job satisfaction and lower job turnover rates. The authors conclude, 'it is very difficult to succeed in contemporary accounting organizations without exhibiting "stereotypic masculine" characteristics; to hold on to a non-masculine orientation appears to be a lonely and difficult path' (Maupin and Lehman 1994: 435).

The study of entrepreneurship has, like other areas of management, paid little attention to gender. While some studies (see for example Goffee and Scase 1985) have helped to illustrate how women's entrepreneurial career paths, experiences and aspirations may differ from men's, adulated entrepreneurial behaviours have typically not been analysed as simultaneous expressions of masculinity.

Two contributors to Collinson and Hearn (1996) address this neglect. Rosslyn Reed's 'Entrepreneurialism and Paternalism in

Australian Management' and Kate Mulholland's 'Entrepreneurialism, Masculinities and the Self-Made Man' offer intriguing dissections of the entrepreneurial psyche and the often fawning ideology of entrepreneurship (see also Kets de Vries 1996). Reed accomplishes this through two case studies of Australian-based publishing entrepreneurs, David Syme and Rupert Murdoch; Mulholland draws on her research of seventy English entrepreneurial families but profiles two contrasting entrepreneurs. Mulholland's chapter excavates the defence of workaholism, including 'presenting effort as sacrifice' (145). She shows how work is used 'to evade deeper involvement with problems associated with family life' (143, and see also Hochschild 1997). Despite family kept at arm's length in both cases, for one entrepreneur an elaborate pretence of commitment to family is central to self-image. One almost preferred the other entrepreneur who made no apologies for not seeing his children for weeks on end because of his work hours.

Both authors reveal the complex gendered constructs of both domestic and organisational division of labour which lies behind the so-called 'self-made' man. Indeed this research ensures we can never again read that phrase—'self-made man'—without questioning the instrumentalism and individualism it lionises. Mulholland cites cases where wives have been founders and active participants in the enterprise but their contributions go unrecognised by the entrepreneurs themselves. In many other cases, entrepreneurs show not even a fleeting recognition that women's single-handed running of families and households has enabled them, in all sorts of ways, to pursue business interests at a consuming level.

A central part of the construction of entrepreneurial masculinity validates self-reliance and independence, the capacity to 'go it alone', while underplaying that these men are consumers of their wives' and families' emotional labour—'recipients of nurturing'. Habits of workaholism and absence from, if not avoidance of, home is made possible because of the power over wives' emotional labour that these men enjoy. Further, such behaviour is lauded, within the ethos of entrepreneurialism, signifying self-sacrifice, discipline and endurance.

Mulholland summarises: 'Husbands' investment in workaholism can often be a disguise for their refusal to engage in emotional work and family responsibilities while they still manage to have leisure time. Exclusive male clubs and male-dominated sports activities constitute the playing ground for many entrepreneurial men' (147). The double load of emotional labour carried by wives of entrepreneurs 'allows men to construct not only their businesses, but also their own masculine self-images' (149).

Even in that bastion of masculinity—the military, Barrett has deconstructed the myth of 'monolithic masculinity' (1996: 129). An overarching navy masculinity has strong resonances with our heroic masculinity of leadership. It 'involves physical toughness, the endurance of hardships, aggressiveness, a rugged heterosexuality, unemotional logic, a refusal to complain'—all attributes tested in 'a culture that chronically creates trials that separate the "weak" from the rest' (132). Yet in different specialisms and levels, particular masculinities are enacted, a product of organisational practices and individual personalities. For example, among pilots the emphasis is on extraordinary levels of risk-taking, boldness and aggressive heterosexual behaviours. At the other end of the hierarchy, among supply officers, technical expertise and power from commanding complex information systems and resources is the basis for masculinity. Barrett observes that despite this textual diversity and a constantly upheld hierarchy among masculinities, all groups are united in their efforts to differentiate themselves from women. Stories of women failing in each occupation are used to bolster exclusivity: 'femininity becomes associated with quitting, complaining and weakness' (1996: 133). When men fail to withstand tests, they are labelled as either 'girls' or 'faggots'. These practices, pervasive at senior officer levels, reveal how redolent in definitions of leadership, become expressions of masculinity.

This description of recent research elaborating managerial masculinities helps to build a more complex, dynamic understanding of the interplay between being an organisational leader and being a man. New aspects and variations are elaborated which provide a deeper and evolving picture of the warrior-like heroism identified in the preceding chapter as the archetype of corporate leadership. However, some ingredients of masculinity built into leadership remain: an urge to conquer, emotional stoicism, physical toughness and endurance—and, underpinning this, a rejection of the feminine and a celebration of maleness through involvement in sporting activities which exclude women.

Alternative Masculinities

Both academic and popular work contains arguments for an expanded and differently shaped masculinity, one that does not rest simply on a rejection of feminine values. Steve Biddulph (1994; 1997), for example, builds a case for a different masculinity which rests on stronger and more expressive bonds between fathers and sons, between male friends and between men and their female partners.

In something of an Australian phenomenon, Biddulph travels the eastern seaboard speaking to packed lecture halls primarily on the subject of masculinity. However, he doesn't call it that. The titles of his seminars and workshops, 'Raising Boys' and 'Love and Discipline', encourage a more publicly palatable focus on parenting. Biddulph's way into helping men reassess themselves is via their relationship with their sons. Talking about the difficulties of parenting boys provides an opportunity for men to begin to unpack themselves, their relationship with their fathers, the reticence and resistances that lie well-buried in their adult selves. Around half of most audiences are men, and they are not only the woollen beanie, vest-clad counter-cultural types. Biddulph draws on his own experience, using a lot of humour and anecdotes to demonstrate his own credentials as a 'real man'.

At the same time, researchers warn us of the dangers of misinterpreting some of this resurgence of alternative male values. Stephen Linstead suggests that 'the New man of the '90s, who adds caring and sensitivity towards partners and children to the panoply of male virtues, is not an overturning of male domination but an elaboration and extension of it'. Thus selective co-option or 'colonization' of 'feminine repertoires' may 're-centre rather than de-centre masculinity and further marginalize the feminine by creating a more "complete" version of masculinity' (1995: 200)

Men Leading Differently

Is this debate, and the emerging research about multiple and alternative masculinities, paving the way for men to pursue a new kind of leadership? In this section I provide some evidence of Australian men leading differently.

Among the male chief executives we interviewed were several who alluded to the 'confusion' men feel about the changed expectations they are experiencing, particularly in their private lives. This may be one reason why many senior men rarely take holidays and maintain long hours at their offices where the badges of their status and authority go unchallenged. This confusion can confound into resentment when women and other men are observed challenging the boundaries of the stereotypical corporate executive.

Another CEO describes new learning processes where male executives took promotions and found themselves miserable. The company now places a much higher value on family issues in shaping executives' careers, and executives can refuse promotions for family reasons and not feel like failures:

> We've had cases where men have taken a promotion and found themselves unhappy in it. We had a guy leave the other day . . . recruited for Hong Kong . . . He was back in a week. He wanted his job back . . . We will leave them where they are for as long as they are happy, especially watching children's age. A change of school can be devastating.

There is also a shift from masculinity as a phlegmatic and solitary toughness to a tentatively nurturant masculinity: executives as men who work and 'interact with peers in a healthy working relationship'. Executives must be 'accessible . . . cheerful, courteous and helpful', 'building people, rather than destroying them with criticism'. Words such as these convey a very different image of executive, and a very different masculinity.

Men are being required to understand their identities as executives in new ways, which include women. In the following extract, one CEO finds parallels between decisions about his own career and those of women in his organisation:

I had to be particularly sensitive about (my comparative youth) and try to build bridges and communicate and try to understand the culture as best I could. And yet I didn't want to give up on trying to change it and bring what I wanted to the party. It was a mixture of continuing to be myself and trying to do, very much to do, the things I believed in and yet trying to understand what it takes to be successful in this environment that doesn't mean total surrender and change and give up . . .

Some of the women, even ethnic minorities . . . have said 'Look I've got to this point; now I look inside and I see what it's going to take to be part of the inner sanctum of this group and I just don't want to do that. I don't want to work like that, or subjugate my person-ality in such a way . . . I'd rather go off on my own, start my own company or go with another company more in tune with my style and values.'

Rick Farley, the former head of the National Farmers Federation, resigned in 1995. At the time, his reasons for resigning and choosing a different kind of life for himself were well publicised, particularly in the radio and print media dominated by women (Doogue 1995; Neales 1996). Farley said of his decision:

I had got to the point in my life where I didn't like what I was becoming. It had become too hard to be mentally tough during the day and mentally soft when I got home. But I couldn't find any other way to do the job that had to be done, without compromising the [NFF] position. (Neales 1996: 22)

When Farley chose to resign, there was much speculation as to the 'real reason' and some veiled implication that he was just not up to the job. Farley responded saying that

It was entirely my own decision to leave because I wanted to change the life I was leading. Any other assertions are incorrect. But I do think when someone like me resigns, it threatens other peoples values . . . to some people what I was doing was the height of their aspirations—so for me to walk away threatens everything they are trying to achieve (Neales 1996: 22)

Farley's reflections on 'other people's values' highlight the powerful reasons why men are reluctant to contemplate and question the way they have chosen to lead. For many people, particularly the more senior and the more successful, too much has been vested in achieving against a particular archetype of masculine leadership.

Significant in Farley's case is that, far from compromising his masculinity, his desire to build a different career and life around his commitment to family and to the Aboriginal groups with whom he was increasingly working was not, initially, marginalised or sniggered at. He was also portrayed as tough and aggressive, a man who has come to know and understand the value of the land. As distinctive Australian heroic myths are strongly rooted in stereotypes of the stoic frontier settler and the laconic boundary rider, Farley's combination of credibilities made it harder for observers to ridicule his decision to forge a new path for himself.

Farley was raised by a mother and grandmother, in relatively modest circumstances and with little contact with his father. In the next chapter we will see how women's upbringing and early experiences can enable them to circumvent narrow societal expectations and gender stereotypes. It might well be suggested that Farley's unusual upbringing fostered a desire to work, lead and live differently. However, subsequent developments have shown the obstacles, not least in the media, to pursuing a non-conventional path to leadership. Farley was recently reported as finding it hard to achieve the outcomes he was seeking, without a high profile and working excessive hours. His relationship with his family had been the casualty (*Age*, 9 June 1997).

Another example of a well-publicised leader opting out of the corporate mainstream is Daniel Petrie, former Vice-President of Microsoft and, before that, Managing Director of Microsoft Australia. Petrie, in an interview with Norman Swan (1996) describes the lure of working with Bill Gates and the extraordinary commitment of hours and energies regarded as normal in the industry. A standing joke at Microsoft was that 'you only work half a day, you decide which twelve hours you will work'. Sleeping at the office and working around the clock were commonplace. But Petrie admits that far from being a burden 'You wanted to be there. You wanted to be part of this'.

Quite early on at Redmond Campus, Seattle, Microsoft's headquarters, Petrie started to have doubts about this pace of work and the toll it was taking. He was the first VP to say 'I am sorry, I can't be there' for a meeting at odd hours of the weekend, and he would tell his staff to go home. The doubts started with the birth of his first child, but then escalated substantially when Petrie's sister died in a car crash in Australia. Always influenced by his sister's model of living, he decided to return to Australia and seek a different kind of success which allowed him to work less hours and spend more time with his children. Among his peers there was disbelief about giving up the opportunity to work with Gates and many expected him to return after an interlude of grieving.

There is, then, anecdotal and very limited evidence of Australian executives pioneering alternative paths. When men question the way they are working it is most typically precipitated by crisis—by impending retirement or retrenchment, by family crisis such as a child going 'off the rails' and demanding men evaluate their parenting, or a wife leaving. In my research I was told how one family influenced their father to modify his habits of working very long hours and travelling frequently. When the father returned from a business trip, the family treated him as an absolute stranger for a sustained period of time. The experience had a quite profound effect on the man, who realised how much he had taken for granted the intimacy of family relationships. From this time on, he reassessed his business and dramatically reduced the time spent at work and travelling.

Another prompt for change can be negotiations with older children and, in particular, adult daughters (for further discussion, see Chapter 8). Children can hold up a mirror to executives, who often see in their adult children a side of themselves which has been repressed or silenced over years of corporate service. For executive men, the demands and experiences of daughters can tap and open their own more feminine side which otherwise goes unexpressed.

For younger men, the birth of children and the demands of dual careers, or even accommodating the more promising and lucrative

career of a partner, can precipitate serious questioning about life priorities. Rick Farley said that for him the turning point came when his
young son asked why he was always so grumpy. Seeing himself
through the eyes of his son, he didn't like the person he had become.
Similarly, for television producer, Steve Vizard, the desire to be part
of his four children's growing up has substantially influenced his work
schedule and priorities.

Re-evaluation can occur if a man's partner transgresses his territory. Women may earn more than their male partner, be stronger,
be a better boss or more capable at negotiating worldly requirements. For some men, this threatens their sense of manliness, though
for others it provides a welcome opportunity to relinquish the
burden of the primary breadwinner role (McKenna 1997).

Men who question traditional notions of masculinity typically do
so because they have to. These are often men with unusual backgrounds coming to terms with particular, sometimes very difficult,
circumstances. Because they rarely have an easy path to a straightforward gender identity and broader identity, gay men often experience a process of actively inspecting and rejecting some masculine
stereotypes, leaving some free to explore different ideas of manhood
(see, for example, Dessaix 1994). We know there are senior executives who are gay, but there are few who are 'out', particularly in
more traditional professions and industries. This underlines the
strength of the unspoken link between masculine heterosexuality and
leadership and the difficulty of leading, as a man, in a different way.

Making Masculinities Visible to Managers

For most men, masculinity continues to be assumed and invisible. It
remains inaccessible for discussion, except in those rare cases where,
due to personal circumstances, it becomes a problem, something that
needs to be changed.

The research I have cited has started to provide ways of talking
about maleness—what it is to be a man. But even if the language
exists, it is my experience that people don't use it until they *feel* issues
or problems and then look for words that will help them explain and
come to grips with what they feel.

In my teaching, with MBA students typically in their late twenties and with more senior managers, there is considerable resistance to contemplating or discussing 'the way men are'. This resistance is magnified if a session devoted to discussion of the masculine culture is short or sandwiched between others on topics that are ostensibly very externally oriented, such as information systems or international management. If a session has been framed as one concerned with gender or diversity, they come prepared to talk about women, not about themselves. My experience, particularly with predominantly male groups, is that the discussion very quickly turns into 'the trouble with women is . . .' Experiences are relayed about no women applying for jobs, about women being unwilling to move interstate, about women working part-time, about them taking a second maternity leave (how dare they!) The desire to scapegoat 'the other' as the problem is overwhelming.

Similarly, in workshop settings with senior managers, unless individuals have had first-hand experience of discrimination or harassment among subordinates, most continue to hold on to the beliefs that there is nothing wrong with the way things are done. If problems are identified, then those problems lie with the women who draw attention to them.

Prompting reflection about masculinities and how they are played out at work is more viable in groups with whom the teacher has developed a relationship, and where there is trust. It is substantially assisted by relaying the experiences and views of other respected men. Quoting leaders like Daniel Petrie and Rick Farley creates a reflective space where men are more willing to talk about their own experiences of feeling trapped, of vulnerability and doubt. Yet there remains an overwhelming sense that this kind of space is an interlude, a deviation from the main business of managing or learning how to be a better manager.

. . .

One form of hegemonic masculinity, a tough and stoic heroism, is pervasive at the senior levels of Australian organisations. Corporate leadership has come to look like this, and those who are unable or unwilling to exhibit this form of masculine heroism, are rarely judged as leaders.

However, the equation of heroic masculinity and leadership is not static. It requires constant demonstration and legitimation in the stories and lessons of leadership that are drawn; in the models of leadership we are encouraged to emulate. Our understandings of masculinities and constructions of leadership are dynamic. Looking at both the research evidence and some examples of senior Australian men, we need to recognise the existence of multiple and changing masculinities. There is a questioning of the heroic archetype. The costs and difficulties of adhering to this aspiration, for men and for women, are increasingly difficult to sustain as dual career couples become the norm and family responsibilities become more genuinely shared.

At the same time, researchers express caution about the notes of optimism that are sounded in relation to new masculinities. The evidence is that experimentation is confined to small groups of men, often those with the economic power to make choices. Meanwhile, the middle and senior levels of large organisations seem to have escaped reflection on these subjects. That men might be seeking more opportunities to discuss relationships with their sons is one thing, but actively engaging in discussion of their own manliness, as demonstrated in and requisite for corporate leadership, is quite another.

When men observe other men leading differently, there is often disbelief, censure, marginalisation, even ridicule. The man trying a new path by, for example, limiting the hours he works, is seen as 'under the thumb' (masculinity compromised by an assertive wife); 'not up to it' (finding an excuse for failure in the big boys' world); or hopelessly diverted and rendered a limp and impotent SNAG (sensitive new age guy).

And we must not be seduced by a masculinity which softens itself at the edges, which learns the language of care and consultation but uses this to strengthen the status quo. The danger is that the 'softer' and more feminine skills of leadership may be learned in order to entrench more deeply the subjugation of women and the superiority of a certain kind of masculinity.

About Women

5 THE MAKING OF LEADING WOMEN: *Early Years*

Through their inherited characteristics, early experiences and family influences, are some women destined to be leaders? Or are they 'made', their leadership forged and earned through a combination of their own abilities and determination with the experiences and opportunities presented to them by life?

Both sets of influences are clearly significant in shaping an appetite for, and career in, leadership. However, I argue that, in the case of women, it is particularly important to recognise the role played by early influences which enable leading women to step outside, or not feel constrained by, social stereotypes of what girls and women do.

Three sets of findings are discussed. Firstly, women leaders tend to exhibit a pattern of parental influence where fathers are regarded affectionately, even adored, while mothers, particularly those who have achieved, are regarded more ambivalently. In some cases this results in women exhibiting and enacting through their leadership lingering desires for paternal approval. In other cases, there is evidence of what psychologists call 'male identification'—a stronger identification with the father than the mother in the shaping of identity. Ambivalence towards their own mothers, particularly ambitious ones, revealed in the chapter, helps us understand the very mixed feelings that female leaders encounter from both female and male subordinates.

The second finding moves to the broader pattern of womens' backgrounds. Women who are leaders have often experienced circumstances which have insulated them from processes of gender stereotyping. They have not, for various reasons, imbibed narrow social stereotypes of what girls and women do and can aspire to do. This insulation might result from a very encouraging, or absent, father; from a highly disrupted childhood or one spent in a remote location; from schooling in which women were the leaders; or some combination of these. Through these circumstances, girls and the young women they become are less saddled with gender stereotypes and expectations which might have encouraged them to censor their aspirations and their self-expression.

Finally, there is some evidence that some female leaders, like their male counterparts, may have experienced some hardship in their childhood which has been a fulcrum of leadership drive and self-reliance. Zaleznik (1977) argues that male leaders are often found to have had solitary childhoods, learning that they don't need others. In contrast to managers who are needy of work companionship and the team's approval, leaders are often loners.

Most studies of leadership make assumptions, explicit or not, about the origins of the leadership character, about the role of 'in born' traits versus learned abilities which enable leaders to rise above the rest. The view that leaders are 'born' emphasises the template of inherited and early experiences which, at a largely unconscious level, endows leaders with an appetite for influence and a conviction that their own vision deserves to serve for others too. The second view assumes that people—by consciously focusing their abilities, ambition and determination and by seeking opportunities and education —can be 'made', and make themselves, into leaders.

In the psychology and management literature, this early theoretical dichotomy took the form of efforts to prove, once and for all, the relative roles of personal traits versus learned competencies (Stogdill 1948). This work acknowledged that some traits were inherited and others acquired. Over subsequent decades, researchers' answers to the question have ebbed and flowed with prevailing orthodoxies. The 'born to rule' and 'great man' theories have suffered in credibility because they have been used to support all sorts of spurious claims justifying élitism, and racial and gender superiority. Several meta-analyses of psychological research have claimed to lay the question to rest (for example, Stogdill 1974; Kirkpatrick and Locke 1991), although, revealingly, it never quite goes away.

Why does the question of how much leaders are born or made seem to resist final resolution? There are several reasons. Firstly, researchers typically have various interests—as do most of us—in believing that, as individuals, we can overcome the shortfalls of our origins. However, when we examine ruling élites, there seems to be a preponderance of people with backgrounds which can be characterised as economically and educationally privileged. Trying to trace the aetiology of leadership through a mass of life factors and forces defies, though continues to tease, researchers.

Secondly, the debate reflects the broader ascendancy of social and economic ideologies. Even in the work of individual leadership theorists, one can plot shifts of emphasis over a lifetime's research. For example, Warren Bennis, one of the most revered observers of leadership, has recently given more emphasis to the view that early experiences and the formation of character traits in early life are important. John Kotter's work, similarly, presents an evolving view which alters over time and depending on its audience for his work. For example, when the audience for published work is more managerial, Kotter's emphasis is on the value to be delivered to potential leaders through training (1990).

For some time it has been unfashionable to emphasise the importance of early experiences in the formation of leadership (Brett 1997). Much of leadership research has a vested interest in believing that leadership is made. For example, a good deal of education is designed to expand young people's appetites and capacities for leadership. If it were found that such capacities were all predestined in the first few years of life, then our efforts might appear more than a little belated.

However, one particular shortcoming of the pervasive view that leaders make themselves is that it does not adequately explain why leadership is gendered. It does not explain why some men can make themselves into leaders, but very few women are seen to do so. It is important to examine early experiences because they shape our understanding of what leadership looks like, and they also shape young people's beliefs about their eligibility for leadership. If, when young, we are only exposed to males in designated leadership roles, then we come to associate maleness with leadership. If we are women, most of us will, consciously or unconsciously, set our sights elsewhere.

I argue that early experiences are important in shaping women's beliefs about leadership, about themselves and their capabilities. Genetic inheritance, in-utero or infant experiences are not included in this analysis of early experiences, but I do include women's re-collections and reconstructions of their childhoods, school years, family environment, adolescence and early work experience.

My research highlights several factors which are important in the experiences of many women who assume leadership roles. A number of women grew up in a family environment which dissuaded or in-sulated them from social stereotypes. For various reasons, these women develop a level of drive, ambition, tenacity and initiative which separates them from others and, again for specific reasons, these qualities are directed towards business or professional achieve-ment. The most commonly reported of these circumstances is a father who imparts to his daughter a strong sense of self and self-confidence that is not gender-tied. Alternatively women have had a mother, either close or distant, who modelled leadership and de-livered a strong contra-stereotyping example.

Later life experiences, from adolescent to adulthood, then propel women to achieve outside family. They are enabled or forced to circumvent or manage the challenge of motherhood and pressures not to outdo husbands. Pivotal circumstances include the influence of a very important mentor; hardship, such as the loss of the security of marriage through death or divorce; or intense exploration of identity issues around sexuality and decisions to have children or not.

The Influence of Fathers

In earlier research of women in politics I found that female leaders often share a particular pattern of perceived parental influence: mothers acting as role models of achievement but frequently am-bivalently regarded; fathers providing a strong sense of daughters' capabilities beyond traditional gender roles (Sinclair 1987).

This pattern is also discernible among the executive women who are the subject of this book. Some fathers endorsed their daughters and made them feel they 'could do anything'. Others were undemanding, but broadly supportive and not perceived as intrusive (as mothers often were). Linda describes the reactions of her 'very working class' father to her appointment as head prefect at high school:

> I think my father was reasonably pleased and, you know, it wasn't a big deal. That was maybe why it was disappointing [long pause] I don't think the family really had a clear idea of what they thought a woman could do . . . My father just was bewildered . . . I just knew he was pleased for me and quite liked the, sort of, reflected glory. I wouldn't call him one of these deeply supportive, soft, generous, nurturing fathers. But he wasn't negative and he is pleased and was pleased . . . it was more just sort of 'goodness me, that's nice'.

Fathers were not always doting of daughters, or even present, but their approval and support was rarely unimportant. In a number of cases, father's approval was infuriatingly unforthcoming—it didn't seem to matter how good the report card or the prize-winning performance. 'Good girl' behaviour by these daughters was simply expected, then passed over, with attention devoted to more troublesome brothers.

Such absence of approval continues to be an important, if unacknowledged, motivation for women to seek situations in which they can become close to, and experience the approval of, powerful men. As mature women they continue to find that their work achievements somehow remain less noteworthy or fail to attract the approval of real and surrogate fathers—although the same men may be more forthcoming when daughters do the womanly thing and provide them with grandchildren (whom they find they can 'enjoy' as they didn't their own children).

Fathers were, in a couple of cases, forgiven for neglect and absence, while mothers were judged more harshly. For example, one woman describes an extraordinarily difficult childhood spent in foster homes, and the eventual premature death of both parents. Neglected by both parents she seized on an account by a neighbour that her father tried to prevent her being fostered. She now finds herself able to forgive him but barely mentions her mother:

. . . they say my father died of a broken heart . . . He married the wrong person, he was in love with someone else . . . It was a tragic story of alcoholism, abuse, broken heart.

Other fathers exert a ghostly presence in their absence, a painful reminder of an early absence or lack of interest which is also a meaningful portent in daughters' lives.

Expectations of fathers in general were lower. Even with a minimum of paternal input, daughters often show fondness or at least tolerance of fathers' foibles and frailties. Mothers, however, were judged against a greater range of benchmarks (work and family) and were often found wanting. Numbers of women described fathers with tenderness—even in the context of fathers' evident lack of interest or preoccupation with other things. In situations where both parents achieved, interviewees are more likely to volunteer pride in being a father's daughter. For example, one woman describes as 'a great honour' the opportunity to give an address about her late father's work.

In a few cases, women's relations with fathers were more testy and combative. These women had spent time coming to terms with feelings of being rejected. However, even where daughters had fiercely separated themselves, fathers and relationships with fathers continue to be influential. Patterns of interaction with fathers become enduring templates of behaviour with later powerful men. One woman describes her way of arresting the attention of her distant, preoccupied father:

. . . being rebellious *in my own way* fairly early on and I guess arguing with my father about things like politics. He was right of Genghis Khan and so I started espousing socialist rhetoric when I was about twelve and having mega fights whilst watching the TV news.

She learned back in the family context some of the challenging behaviour involved in her current role. And there certainly seems to be satisfaction in that, despite sharing the same management field as her father, she judges her contribution much the better.

Mothers: From Ambivalence to Muted Admiration

Mothers are often regarded with ambivalence by the women in my research. If they've been successful or had a public profile, there can be resentment about mothers putting themselves first. If mothers have been homemakers and more circumspect in their ambitions, there's often impatience and a trace of contempt for these mothers who haven't asserted themselves enough, or have lined up too obligingly behind father's authority in the family. While fathers provoke tenderness or resentment, some mothers get barely a mention. I often needed to ask very explicit questions to hear about some mothers.

One woman with an illustrious history of strong and famous women in her family seems notably unmoved by their activities. Instead, it is her father's achievements she recalls with great tenderness and pride. Another comes right out and says, 'My mother was a strange woman. I have no idea what my father really saw in her'.

Ruth can barely bring herself to describe the decline of her father—from a man in uniform, much travelled and adored when he was home, to a man who paled as he grew into middle-aged ineffectualness. Through this period it was her mother who, pulling herself up from lowly origins, made a success in small business. Yet mother's model is not so glowingly described—this women can see, if she detaches herself, that her mother's career was a very considerable achievement, but she is not moved by it, as she was by her handsome father's adventures then fading demise into middle-age.

At the extreme were those mothers whose own aspirations had been thwarted and contained by circumstances. In their daughters' eyes they often seem like inadvertent competitors. One interviewee describes her mother studying high-school subjects at the same time as herself. The daughter's reaction was to effectively 'drop out' of this area, in which she had been 'a top student'. She describes her mother as 'ambivalent' about her own success—neither wanting her daughter to stay a homemaker nor strongly supportive of her current lifestyle. She speculates that the cause was her mother's underlying frustration: 'I think she's never quite felt fulfilled even though she certainly did a great deal more than other women in her era.'

Mothers who have provided 'role models of women working' generally receive support. At the same time, mothers are supposed to put children first and to fit their own aspirations around their children's needs. Not surprisingly, there are not many mothers who are seen to get this delicate balance right. They are either a bit neglectful, self-serving and rivalrous, on the one hand, or prone to martyrdom on the other. The patterns of these perceptions are important not just for what they say about these particular daughters' experiences, but for what they tell us about attitudes to women with power in general. Such ambivalence exists, even among these women who are reflective about their own experiences as women with authority.

While working mothers are an intellectual model for aspiring female leaders, daughters often want to escape the confines of mothers' occupations. A number of mothers, facing highly constrained career options, had taken up teaching. Interviewees who had followed this path couldn't wait to get out:

> I thought I am not going to do Arts and just be an arts person, I want to do economics and be a business person . . . An arts person was more like my mother and a business person was more escaping from that. So I did economics and then did teaching [laughs] Well, I tried not to, you know . . . I can remember ringing a couple of companies who had bursaries and so on . . . but I just didn't have the capacity to penetrate that world at that age.

Working mothers do demonstrate that girls can aspire to serious work roles, but in other ways these girls want to differentiate from mothers, using alternative careers to do so. None of the interviewees' mothers had anything like an easy path combining work and mothering, and some daughters felt the sharpness of a mother's envy. This emotional subtext works in very complex ways, with daughters seeking to be successful as career women yet needy of support from mothers and feeling cheated when it is not forthcoming. At the same time, daughters' successes and their opportunities to sustain career through mothering often make their mothers feel cheated too, realising what they may have had to give up.

The experience of the interviewees highlights that, first and foremost, women are judged against a maternal norm—they are expected to support and be selfless. These mothers and daughters, some of whom have daughters themselves, are thus negotiating deeper and more treacherous territory before they reach the more separate and respectful relationship that sometimes occurs between fathers and daughters.

Female Role Models

All interviewees volunteered the importance of female role models. These are teachers, often nuns, family members, early bosses or, more rarely, mothers who are determined and self-reliant. These role models show it can be done, that women can have an influence on the world.

In Angela's case there is a strong matriarchal tradition. She volunteers her mother as a role model and spells out how her mother and other women in her family have made their mark by being different:

> . . . certainly my mother was a role model. She was one of the few mothers in my street that went back to work, in fact she went back and got an education . . . she went and got a degree in psychology and, you know, it was like she was different to the other mothers for that reason, and I thought that was pretty good . . . it was interesting having a mother that worked. I thought it was good. In fact I always wanted to be a school teacher which was what she was . . . up until I became a school teacher and realised how awful that was [laughter]. All the women in my family . . . have got a mixture. They are strong and often single and had to go against the world to look after themselves . . . the men have all died or sort of had crises or whatever and there is not a strong male role model in my family at all.

It is worth noting that Angela's mother was never a real competitor. Like most in the sample, the interest of these mothers in their adult daughters' success is limited. This may be a protection against envy. Given the dramatic change in opportunities for women over the last generation, mothers might be expected to have mixed feelings about the opportunities they perceive are available to their daughters, opportunities to have both a successful career and a family.

Childhood memories reveal circumstances in which women imbibed high expectations for themselves from father or mother and it didn't seem to occur to them to compromise abilities or aspirations to conform to ideas of what young women should do. One, who was the top student in her undergraduate, male-dominated profession says simply, 'It was always expected that I would, it was always assumed I would do well'. And she notes that she didn't 'find it hard to do well, enjoyed it'.

Although mothers are regarded with some ambivalence, in a pattern that is consistent with my argument, executive women have very frequently had female role models from somewhere. Teachers are cited, particularly at all-girls schools. These schools frequently provide an environment relatively free of inhibitions, where girls have a go at many things, test boundaries and try themselves out without feeling observed or judged by male peers or elders. One describes her experience as captain at a girls high school:

> [It was] a very very good school in that it really encouraged girls to do whatever you were good at . . . I was a very fat teenager and I had eating problems basically [her parents were divorcing at this stage] But I remember being totally outrageous in that Year 12 concert, the school captain being the talk of the town . . .

Another woman, 'the only migrant child' at a girls high school, eventually 'won the English prize at school in my final year'. She describes the impact of a woman teacher who managed to combine nurturance and modelling achievement with being 'gorgeous':

> I had a wonderful English teacher who encouraged me . . . she taught me that communication in writing is very easy . . . I also learned about blue eyeshadow and blue mascara. She wore blue mascara and had the most gorgeous blue eyes. She was a mentor and all sorts of things.

It is frequently through school that young women learn that women can lead, can be both strong and womanly (even though, when they experience that strength and commitment to work in their own mothers, they don't necessarily like it).

Female colleagues or bosses less often provide role models. This may say much less about the willingness and capacity of women to act as role models than about the rarity of women in positions of authority. But, particularly for women at an early stage of career, the impact of a more senior woman confidante can be very considerable. When Susan got a job in a very traditional male transport company, she had the benefit of working closely with the only other professional woman in the organisation:

> The way Mary operated was that she would watch me train and then at the end of it she would de-brief every second of it. Then you would go 'Okay, did that work?' 'No, what would have been better?' 'Right!' So it was that. 'Okay, I think you need to go on an assertiveness training course . . . She presented a few models of behaviour, to help me . . . She sort of lived the message a bit . . . Then she moved to another organisation and I found that very difficult. I found that I lost, I felt a sense of loss of my female self very strongly.

Male Mentors and Models

In early career, the support of men is a consistent theme. They may be husbands or friends, who helped the younger woman make her transition from being defined as the daughter to an independent woman.

Older male managers can be either models or mentors. Men employed in the same organisation can be effective sponsors, providing advice, encouragement and opportunities to women. The older man often gets satisfaction and feels flattered in guiding a young woman's career, and typically the young woman is respectful and grateful for his help. This strongly paternal/filial relationship may not last, particularly if women become successful enough to appear as competitors, or if they stop so graciously accepting advice. A difficult transition may accompany women accepting promotions—they move from having the support of senior males to feeling suddenly deserted and isolated. However, in some cases relationships endure through the woman ageing and becoming increasingly successful, particularly if her mentor retires or moves on and there is no threat of competition.

Other bosses show how to be a different kind of leader. In this woman's account of an early, much admired boss, is a picture of how she wants to be:

> . . . he was very innovative, he didn't care for convention very much . . . he himself had a very unconventional life style which he didn't make a secret of . . . He was a senior executive and people knew and it was just too bad if they didn't like it.

It is often men who define for women their eligibility for leadership. Women tend not to think of themselves in these terms until an older male recognises ability and demonstrates confidence. In my research on women undertaking MBAs, I also found evidence that women needed the catalyst of men's encouragement before they felt eligible to enrol. Their first response was to think: '*I* couldn't do that' (Sinclair 1995a). Although it is regrettable that this should be so, these findings highlight the importance for women of having male mentors, particularly at formative stages of career.

Hardship Leading to Self-Reliance

A number of women had experienced quite substantial setbacks and hardship as children. Sustained illness or stays in hospital, family break-ups and solitary childhoods nurtured in some a fierce self-reliance and a capacity to fend for themselves early:

> I was away from home when I was very young, on and off for eighteen months to two years . . . I came home different, independent, unattached to my family . . . with tremendous determination . . . I went away a sort of fluffy little girl and came home very strong. I'd lost a lot of the soft femininity from my persona . . . I was either going to go down the tube and get sick and be depressed or I was going to come up fighting. When my psychology allowed me to come up fighting, I think I remained that way.

As the only child of older and rather distracted parents, Anna found a similar self-reliance. A small all-girls school couldn't offer all subjects so Anna and her friend 'taught ourselves . . . she and I did maths together, and physics and chem. Virtually taught ourselves for the last two years of school'. She believes that much of the 'strength of [her] generation' came from 'this taste of the obstacles . . . they just had to survive by themselves and they have'.

In her study of female managers 'moving on', Judi Marshall (1995a) makes the point that women's careers are often born out of, of forged through, difficult circumstances, such as opposition from families or personal setbacks. Marshall gives the example of one woman who, though academically very able, was sent to secretarial college by an uninterested father, while her brother was sent to Cambridge.

One way or another, most of the women in my sample describe themselves as 'loners' or, if not loners, then accustomed to their own company and highly self-reliant. While this does not mean they don't enjoy, and excel at, leading teams, they need this independence to survive the experience of ascending to a senior role. And the bases of these qualities seem to lie, at least partially, in their early experiences.

. . .

The backgrounds of female leaders reveal a combination of circumstances in which, as girls, these women were encouraged to believe that they 'could do anything'. Through a variety of circumstances, they didn't imbibe the narrowly circumscribed aspirations for women that were pervasive at the time. In the next two examples, the interweaving of influences is highlighted.

For Andy, a father's regard, mother's ambition, young years spent with grandmother and aunt as role models and a small but progressive girls school combined to nurture confidence in herself and a resulting refusal to be narrowed by gender stereotypes or traditional expectations:

> We were a small family, two girls. My father treated us as equals. We didn't ever feel that we weren't equal to young men growing up. We were enouraged to be independent, independent thinking . . . It was very hard. We didn't do a lot of things others did and my parents took all their money to send us two girls to grammar school . . . He used to make suits at night to pay the school bills . . . But I did live with my grandmother and aunt down here in Melbourne for some years while they were trying to make a go of the business

in the country. My grandmother was totally uneducated but very creative and very musical and so I was encouraged with the painting and colour and music and all those sort of things . . . They sent us down here [to Melbourne] to school because they said there weren't any decent schools where they lived. That was mother but I thank her very much for that because it was a wonderful school. I loved it. Had a go at everything and we were encouraged to do everything.

This woman goes on to describe her early career as a commercial artist when her ability and an award ensured that she was paid as much as a rather pompous relation.

Encouraging fathers and/or strong mothers can nurture in their daughters a set of aspirations for themselves unbounded by stereotypical notions of the roles women should play. The influence of fathers and mothers unfolds in very different ways and arouses different responses—there is more affection and forgiveness in women's accounts of their fathers and more ambivalence and distance in accounts of mothers.

In Nora's case, 'a tough, penniless' background and the difficulties of enduring the 'cruelty' of other children's ridicule at being different, forged a strong individuality and a capacity 'to learn very quickly'. Although both parents were important, it was her father's model which was critical to future career: 'I learned at his feet, as it were'. She worked by her father's side from quite a young age. This background, combined with attending an enlightened girls school and the support of female teachers enabled this woman to succeed at university in a very traditionally male discipline.

While no single ingredient of background could be described as indispensable, and keeping in mind the smallness of this sample, there are some discernable patterns which deserve comment. The differential contribution made by fathers and mothers to their daughters' aspirations is notable. Mothers show how it can be done while fathers are more likely to instil a confidence or belief in oneself. Mothers inspire by example—of working and/or managing a family. In a survey of forty-seven Western Australian women academics and general university staff, mothers were twice as likely as fathers to be volunteered as a guide and role model.

Mothers are admired and sometimes regarded affectionately, but ambivalence is also common. Even among the group of high achieving women that I interviewed, there remain unresolved pressures about where a woman's priorities should lie—with family or work. As adults, these women can appreciate mothers' achievements, but there are resentments and a sense of being displaced as children themselves which continue to be felt into adulthood.

This finding adds further evidence to the proposition advanced in Chapter 2 about how female authority is viewed and how women face extra burdens in establishing their authority in leadership because of relations with mothers. To understand the idealisation of male power and the problems we have with maternal power we need to acknowledge the impact of our earliest exchanges with mothers and fathers (Dinnerstein 1978; Grieve and Perdices 1981; Iseman 1981).

The importance of schooling and, in particular, girls schools which expect leadership and self-reliance is another pattern to emerge from this sample. Schools were a fertile source of female role models and empowering experiences for some young women. They provided an environment where girls weren't competing with boys and where they were expected to take on intellectual and leadership challenges without risking comparisons with boys or, worse, the ridicule and intense self-consciousness that often accompanies puberty.

Finally, mentors nourish self-confidence, particularly in early career. A mentor can plant the seeds of a woman's sense of her eligibility for leadership, which if left to her own devices she might never acknowledge or act on. The most important thing a mentor can do is say, in one way or another, 'you could do that' or 'why don't you try it'. Mentors can be bosses or friends, fathers or partners. But, as with other factors, a mentor is a welcome but not essential ingredient in women's apprenticeships to leadership.

In a recent survey of Australian leaders, both male and female, a high proportion volunteered their early experiences as critically important in the shaping of careers (Sarros and Butchasky 1996). While it is not a particularly fashionable emphasis in leadership research, the argument of this chapter is that, when we are considering the emergence of female leaders, we need to give particular attention to backgrounds.

Research tells us that the formation of sex-role stereotypes and ideas about what boys do and what girls do begins at an early age, in families and with friends, in kindergartens and primary schools. Because relatively few women have been recognised as leaders, and because women are often reluctant to recognise leadership in themselves, we need to understand the experiences of those who seem to be exceptions. This research suggests that female leaders have experienced a range of circumstances in their childhood and early adulthood which have enabled them to have high, and often unconventional, expectations of themselves—as well as the drive and confidence to take on challenges.

6 OBSTACLES TO WOMEN ACQUIRING POWER

Establishing leadership and authority in a senior management role is more complex for women than for most men. This chapter examines why this is so, focusing on the systemic and structural barriers which make it difficult for women simultaneously to establish authority as leaders and maintain their identity as women.

Women in corporate leadership trangress societal expectations —that authority figures are men and that women's realm is the private, family domain. My findings reveal that establishing themselves in a leadership role is, for women, an ongoing struggle in which their sex and their difference are often in the foreground of people's response.

That they are often doing leadership in a different way, and are seen to be different, introduces extra obstacles and additional negotiations. Women in leadership roles are also often operating with a lower level of background support than many male colleagues experience. Rather than enjoying societal endorsement and recognition, women frequently encounter censure and disapproval. Families and friends may exhibit resentment, which explains why women are often prompted to look elsewhere, for example to professional networks, to find endorsement for their career choices.

In her study of twelve middle to senior female managers 'moving on', Judi Marshall (1995) identifies a range of challenges including relating to other powerful people; isolation and being tested out; relating to other women; operating as change agents; experiencing constraints versus enjoying power and influence, and managing self. Marshall concludes from these findings that 'creating a viable and self-congruent identity and finding ways to exercise power are significant challenges for many women' (1995b: 25).

There are many models which categorise obstacles women experience in senior roles and test for the relative impact on aspirations and careers of various obstacles. Still (1993) provides an excellent summary of much of this research (see also Bellamy and Ramsay 1994). Rather than aiming for comprehensiveness or replicating relative obstacles, the seven issues discussed in this chapter reflect the particular tensions experienced by the senior women I interviewed in fitting into the leadership category—a category defined, as we have discussed, with men in mind. They are:

- the look of leadership—conflicts of style;
- pressures for conformity and camouflage;
- sexualisation of women in the workplace;
- maternalisation of women in authority;
- getting administrative support;
- responses from family and friends;
- loss of self, body and sexuality.

The first five of these issues are the product of a pervasive social and workplace discomfort with women in authority. Women in leadership roles often 'come across' to audiences as different—they evoke different feelings and expectations, which women then have to devise strategies for handling. The last two issues are concerned with the impact of these challenges on women leaders' sense of themselves.

The Look of Leadership: Conflicts of Style

Most women I have spoken to, in the formal sample or more informally, are loathe to describe themselves as leaders. One interviewee, a CEO, stated explicitly what a number of others hinted at:

> I'm not at the top. I mean I'm head of a really creative, exciting organisation, but I mean I'm not at the top of anything . . . I don't think you're talking to a proper CEO. I think that's some of the problem with this interview . . . I mean a proper CEO is somebody who is really drivingly ambitious. I mean I'm driving to go and create something valuable . . . or you know, I don't know what I'm driving towards but it's something like that. That's not exactly the same [as the authentic 'driving', ambitious CEO].

Asked whether she considers herself chief executive material, Katherine is reticent, recognising that 'I think probably that I have the capacity' but that 'I probably still seem as being a bit young'. She describes attending a training course which 'separated people into Thinker, Doer, Leader and Carer . . . and the guy running the course thought I was a thinker and carer rather than a leader'. On reflection she feels that she is a leader but that other men expect leaders to be marked by assertiveness and decisiveness:

> I think the men prefer someone decisive, they prefer you to be decisive and wrong than spending too long weighing up the issues . . . my style is very much to sort of seek views from people, see all the subtleties as a problem . . . and taking time to make a decision. So that is probably a personality trait that most of the men are not quite so comfortable with . . . it is probably a couple of years away where the opportunity would arise again [to be considered for CEO] and the reality is I probably don't have the capacity to do it with the children being so little, probably a pretty thankless task as well. [But would you like to do it, take on CEO?] Yes I would like to do it, just to demonstrate to myself I could do it and do it well, which I think I could.

Here is a very real reluctance to label oneself a leader. One widely held explanation for this response has been the view that women share a 'fear of success'. An original study by Horner (1972) found that when asked to write stories on the basis of initial cues, women's stories contained far more obstacles and anticipated conflict than men's. These original findings were later widely misused to argue that women were inevitably more fearful and without the requisite ambition to succeed.

Several more powerful reasons why women are often reluctant to identify themselves as leaders emerge from these and other interviews. Katherine has too many perjorative connotations of leadership to put herself in this category. She cannot identify with 'being on top' for the sake of it and the 'driving' commitment which she associates with leadership. Leadership, for her, fails to include the activities and concerns which she adopts in her role—what she does.

And she expresses some frustration that how she operates as a leader is different enough to be judged by the trainer and by her peers as not exhibiting leadership characteristics. This represents another reason for women's reluctant connection with leadership.

A number of other women use the size of their organisation, the fact that it is not-for-profit or a professional partnership, to distance themselves from the mantle of leadership—to assert in effect that 'what I do is not really leadership'. Instead they often recast what they do using a language and set of ideas with which they are more comfortable. Clearly the conventional discourse of leadership* is one with which many women in senior positions do not readily connect.

A further factor is exemplified in Katherine's modesty about judging herself as leader material. As research supports, women tend to undervalue their performance. A complaint often made is that women 'don't blow their own trumpet enough'. Yet women's experience is that if they do so, they are judged harshly and against a lower benchmark of acceptable self-promotion than male colleagues. In effect, women are expected to be more modest. Katherine avoids sounding boastful, qualifying her accomplishments in the way women do: 'I think probably I have the capacity', while later asserting her desire and capacity to 'do it'.

I have argued throughout this book that the language of leadership is not one to which women are immediately attracted or with which they readily associate. We should not draw from this the conclusion that women are ill-suited to leadership roles. Rather we need to examine the way internalised constructs of leadership have evolved to exclude women and women's experience. Women's preferences and skills in leading have often been neglected in treatments of leadership (for example, the leadership of women in voluntary and not-for-profit organisations), or have been marginalised.

When women experience conflicts between their leadership style and those adopted by the men around them, it is important for us and them to understand, at a deeper level, the reasons for those differential perceptions.

---

* For a discussion of discourses and discourse in the construction of leadership and accountability see Sinclair (1995c; 1996a).

Pressures for Conformity and Camouflage

The way in which senior management cultures, designed and developed to suit men, impact on women has been widely documented (for example Marshall 1984 and 1993a; Gordon 1991).

My interviews similarly reveal the frustration women experience in trying to work within an environment which men, on the whole, support and derive satisfaction from. Elizabeth is wrestling with her different circumstances and the lack of recognition from her workplace that she has two young children:

> . . . most of the people who work here are men . . . who have wives who don't work . . . So most of the men are highly supported in home environments . . . I don't think they contemplate that I am different from them and I think that is possibly a good thing. Although from time to time I feel like screaming at them, 'Have you got any idea what the real world is like? What I have done in order to get here to this early morning meeting!'

Later she refers to an extended period where both her young children were ill and she and her husband worked shifts—the husband waking at 3 a.m. and working till lunchtime and she going to work when he came home, finishing at 10 or 11 p.m.

In this quote and example, Elizabeth feels that camouflaging her status as mother, not recognising her difference, may be the best course. A clear separation between her work self and family self offers the prospects of her being treated on her own 'merits'. However, the hidden inequities of this approach, of pretending that she, like most of her male colleagues, comes to work supported and free of other worries, at times provokes huge frustration.

Most women have actively sought to minimise the impact of child-bearing on their organisations. More than one have fitted having babies into annual leave, taking no maternity leave. Many have found ways of working while on leave. Women are frequently encouraged by peers to feel that by taking more than minimum leave they will be 'letting the side down' and are showing a lack of commitment to the organisation.

Many of the pressures to conform are unspoken and invisible, but palpable and very difficult to resist. Angela describes them:

> There is an expectation around hours and I want to have a balanced life, so there is a lot of pressure on that, which I try not to get hooked into but sometimes that is difficult, you know. I need to exercise, I can't function if I don't, which means leaving work at six . . . well that is okay, it is passable, but 6.30 or 7.00 is better . . . But others work a routine which I can't, which I hate . . . really really long hours, that sort of stuff. It will wear me down.

The pressures to conform to the ways of being and working offered in this culture are very strong. Assessments about one's commitment, abilities and performance are more often tied to demonstrated observance of the cultural rituals than other more objective tests. It is hard for women to hold on to a sense of their own contribution when the organisation consistently fails to recognise what they do as being leadership.

Seeking a move from a marketing role in the company to an executive role, one woman describes the difficulties in getting her boss to understand her motivation and to appreciate that her way of working might be different to most of her male colleagues. He was 'astounded' by her request to talk about her options, judging that the long hours and her general willingness to take work on were evidence of her enjoyment of the job, rather than her professionalism. His response was to judge that she was failing and looking for a reason to move to a less demanding role. The more she tried to explain, the more she perceived an inability on his part to appreciate her motivators:

> I wanted to get into something I enjoyed more, had some prospect of being better at or efficient at, and getting the hours down, and be more manageable, than just being in the office hour after hour—it looks good even if its long-term counterproductive. But he really didn't get it at all. In the end I decided that it didn't really matter if he got it or not. The important thing was I got what I wanted. So I just let it go.

Sexualisation of Women in the Workplace

A number of the women interviewed were the first in their organisation to be in a managerial role. In some industries and organisations, harassment and debasement of women was well entrenched. One woman tells of her experience of attending a celebratory Christmas lunch with her male colleagues and noticing a table of women alongside them: 'I never thought anything about this table of women until I was told that they were prostitutes who had been hired for their entertainment after lunch. I left!' In these and similar experiences, women are not only being isolated. They are being 'tested' by being told or made aware of what is going on.

A middle manager described a long-standing Friday ritual of lunching at a 'table top dancing' venue. Numbers of her male subordinates regularly attended, arriving back at work boisterous and a bit boozed. Some seemed to take some pleasure in making it clear where they had been, volubly describing and disparaging the dancers' bodies. Not very senior at this time, she was at a loss to know how to deal with this behaviour, which was not just tolerated by the organisation but in which a number of more senior managers participated. Although she tried to ignore it, she was surprised at how much it affected her, professionally and personally.

Even if women work hard to model professional ways of working with men in the workplace, circumstances like these are designed, consciously or unconsciously, to remind the woman of her status as sex object and to reduce her power. She is made to feel not just an interloper but reducible to her sex, sometimes an inferior representative of her sex or a member of a sex that is contemptible—valued as a body and only briefly as that.

Comments which ostensibly compliment women on their 'coping' often have a double-edged impact. For example, among the interviewees are several who have fitted mothering into senior careers, sometimes taking babies to work or to meetings when they can be confident the baby will cause no disruption. Male colleagues have said, 'Isn't she marvellous' and make similar comments, perhaps unaware that such continual highlighting foregrounds a woman's role as mother and often marginalises her contribution to the business at hand.

A presentation to senior directors was described by another interviewee. She argued the need to bring more emotion and passion into the way the business was run. A male colleague suggested she look under the table and between their legs if she wanted to see passion. In another example, the process of women participating in a supposedly objective and 'merit-driven' interview process was transformed into a sexualised beauty pageant by male interviewers, with applicants given a ranking on a sexual scorecard, behind their backs. Interviewees have been asked 'How's your sex life', often unexpectedly, publicly and by colleagues with whom they thought they had a good working relationship.

Particularly early in their career, some women encountered a prevalent ethos of affairs between powerful men and subordinate women—an accepted institutionalisation of gender relations. When women progress to managerial roles, the expectation is that they will submit to the same sexual norms, particularly if they are single. One interviewee described an environment in which she, along with other unattached women, were assumed to be 'fair game':

> Of course there is a huge amount of that going on . . . women like
> *me* were always sort of fair game, considered to be fair game . . . my
> perception was I was considered to be a desirable candidate for an
> affair, particularly by senior married men, because I was un-
> attached, enigmatic, those sorts of things. I am not saying that about
> just me in particular. Any intelligent woman in the corporate setting
> who appears to be unattached is considered to be a candidate for an
> affair.

Maternalisation of Women in Authority

As they become older and more senior, women in the workplace become a different kind of threat to some men. Accustomed to judging and dismissing women on the basis of their sexual attractiveness, some men have great difficulty dealing with more mature women simply as colleagues or bosses.

Sometimes this takes the form of discomfort and real repugnance. One interviewee spoke about a friend, another CEO, who was having difficulties with a very senior man in her organisation:

> She couldn't play any of the roles he wanted. He likes women who are tame . . . and this woman certainly wasn't that. She's a strong woman and she can't, in her physical appearance or emotional style, please him.

In other cases, there is overly dependent behaviour, from both men and women. The residues of family dynamics continue to contaminate employees' interactions with bosses, and seniority is no protection. In Linda's view this happens in male-led organisations where women can become overly needy of feedback, and she points to the rarity of female leaders in arguing that the bases of some men's difficulties with female bosses may similarly lie in family contexts.

> I've seen it where women have badly wanted their CEO or their manager to give them feedback and when they don't get it, they get beside themselves . . . They've never had adequate support from their fathers and they expect it from the workplace . . . They're not necessarily going to feel very comfortable at work until they become less dependent. I don't see why it wouldn't be the same with men. I think with women, it's just that there are so few of us, it's a shock and some men can't bear it, they simply can't bear it.

Women who are subordinates to female bosses can also experience mixed feelings. There is the well-documented expectation that women be more understanding, more tolerant, more sensitive than their male colleagues. Women will sometimes accept authority and direction more readily from men, because they are accustomed to it. They may be more likely to be suspicious of a female leader's credentials, perhaps regarding her as a competitor, and they may regard suspiciously any ways of managing that deviate from the norm.

Women in positions of authority act as magnets for unconscious and often unresolved feelings about women in general and mothers in particular. As discussed in Chapter 2, this occurs regardless of how women lead, regardless of how professionally they behave. It is not a function of women's behaviour but rather the novelty of the relationship—female boss and male or female subordinate—and the deep and unexplored feelings this can evoke. Men describe working with a woman in authority as reminding them of their kindergarten teacher. In one recent case, a female money-market manager successfully alleged discrimination by her employer when she was referred to as 'a mother hen', her department as 'the nursery' and the 'mother's club'. This was alongside a sexist dealing-room culture in which there was also consistent sexualisation of women. The organisation's response, despite the substantial pay-out ($135 000) to the complainant, was to regard the incident as 'isolated' and view disciplining the managers involved as 'unneccessary'.

Of course, not all men or women react to female leaders in this way. Sometimes men who have experienced strong but loving mothers and other female role models are much more comfortable with the relationship. Women bosses try to deal with these tensions through very careful selection of subordinates. In particular they seek out men who, for various reasons, seem comfortable with their own masculine identity and are not threatened by women: 'they're not macho, go-getting, ruthless types'.

Getting Administrative Support

Although most workplaces have reduced the amount of secretarial and administrative support available to senior executives, the most senior typically still enjoy a full-time personal assistant who, in some cases, 'runs their [work] lives'. For both the senior executive and the supporting woman, this is a well-understood relationship.

A number of the female interviewees are ably supported by their office staff. However, for reasons described in this book and elsewhere, women in authority positions often evoke greater unease and ambivalence among support staff—male and female. The arrangement of female bosses and male secretaries both transgresses social expectations and traverses unfamiliar gender relations. Relations between executive women and support staff often evoke anxieties and require deliberate investment of effort and skilful negotiation to successfully establish and maintain. Sometimes senior women find that they share secretarial or administrative staff, or they have access to general office staff. In practice, this means negotiating with support staff to have their work given priority. Where it is competing against the work of senior men, women sometimes find that their work and their needs are given a lower priority because of unspoken norms that women should do such things for themselves.

Gendered hierarchies in the workplace take a long time to break down. Pringle (1988) has shown how the relationship between male bosses and female secretaries is supported by societal conventions, in some cases becoming a kind of workplace 'marriage'. Female bosses disturb these gender hierarchies, and the relationship a senior woman builds with her support staff involves much new learning, on both sides—learning which has to swim against entrenched stereotypes.

Responses from Families and Friends

Women who pursue a high-level corporate career are doing something different. This inevitably attracts attention and is not always welcomed by family and friends, who would often rather not have to share the woman's time and emotional energies. Concern expressed by family for her health and well-being can be experienced by the woman as criticism, not support, for her decision to have a career.

For women with young children the pressures are inevitably acute. Many describe longings when children are small to be 'a stay-at-home mum'. However good the child-care arrangements, women are constantly having to adjust patterns of working to accommodate changing children's needs. And the particular processes by which society holds women more responsible than men for the emotional and physical health of children have been widely canvassed. All this leads to what one senior partner in a consulting and accounting firm describes as two sorts of guilt. Her view is that fathers have clearer boundaries separating them from their children. They will certainly ensure that children are safe and comfortable, but they have clearly defined limits about what they can 'fix' and what is up to the child. Women, in contrast, often feel that they have never done enough, that their children's problems are their problems, and that if children struggle or fail it is mother's fault.

While most women argue the need for girls to have career role models, in personal terms this can be difficult to sustain. One woman's primary school daughter said to her that she 'wished her teacher could be her mummy'. Another daughter, watching as her mother was doing her hair to go to work, said 'I don't like the work mum. I much prefer the home mum'. There is little sustenance here for women trying to combine being a female leader and a different kind of mother.

Most women in my sample find that their family, however supportive in a personal sense, has limited tolerance and interest in their work and its challenges. As discussed in the preceding chapter, women often find that their own mother provides intermittent support at best, rather than being the doting backstop for which they had optimistically hoped. Grandparents can be reluctant child-carers, increasingly likely to be preoccupied with their own work and interests and to be geographically mobile. In another form of the double standard described earlier, grandmothers are expected to be nurturers. Women leaders share this expectation with the rest of society. Yet their relationships with their own mothers are often over-laid with small resentments and rivalries and grandmothers are understandably wary about sacrificing their own lives to re-live the task of child-rearing. One result is that few women receive whole-hearted support from parents, particularly mothers, when they try to juggle family and career.

With the exception of a few senior women, who may be living with older or semi-retired partners, most don't get a strong sense of endorsement about their work, nor are they forgiven for being pre-occupied or working long hours. Female partners and close female friends in similar corporate roles are more frequently confidantes about work issues. The hunger that professional women feel for endorsement and encouragement in their difficult 'juggling act' is undoubtedly one of the reasons why women's networks have thrived.

Loss of Self, Body and Sexuality

I have described the male executive journey as a heroic one in which stoicism and toughness are highly valued. In a highly competitive environment, described by many as a battle, there is little room for men to show different sides of themselves as men. The vulnerable, nurturing, family-oriented, expressive and artistic sides of men are

effectively censored from expression in most organisational environments. Yet if a man follows this path, there is much to be gained—a
sense of purpose and status, the respect of other men, a clear and
socially endorsed identity.

The struggle for women is different. Angela describes her experience in a transport company where, as one of very few managerial women, she suffered high visibility and a consequent loss of
herself:

> . . . in that male environment, there was no room for me to be who
> I was . . . because a lot of attention was given to me being a woman
> anyway . . . visually you stand out because you are different. So
> there is that. The focus is always on that you are different, and there
> is no value on that difference really . . . I would often say 'I have lost
> my body', I feel I have lost my female self.

She draws a parallel between this work experience and an extended
stay in Pakistan where she lived within an insulated family environment:

> I had lost my body because of the environment, the male environ-
> ment, and you have to cover yourself, you know, you were not
> allowed to express anything.

Women described how they learned to censor talk of their family in business contexts and how they experienced this, in extreme
instances, as a kind of schizophrenic identity. One, the only female
member of the senior management team, said:

> If we have drinks and I say something about the kids, it just drops
> like a stone. They don't know what to do with it . . . I used to think
> that on occasions like that we would really find out what is happen-
> ing. But top management teams aren't close. I find out more about
> what's happening through the secretaries.

. . .

Women find it hard, on the whole, to talk comfortably about their
leadership. When I asked a question about this in interviews, it
became clear that many understood leadership as a process and a
state already defined by the men who had gone before them. There

was not a ready match with their own aspirations and what they understood as leadership:

> I have a perception that being 'leadership material', which in this organisation means being promoted the next level to Managing Director, is very much like joining the club. I mean, it is down to the selection process . . . literally, people sit around and talk about people's personal qualities. I mean it is just like joining the Melbourne Club.

Leadership comes ready-defined for executives. But it is a construction more likely to reflect men's aspirations and understandings than women's. Many of the interviewees define what they want to do in their work in opposition to the trappings of 'leadership' as defined by the organisation. For example, they say that they want to enjoy the work. When they look to male managing directors or CEOs they often judge that leadership, as currently defined, involves sacrifice of how they want to work and what they are working for.

Much of the managerial research has misconstrued women's reticence about leadership, deducing that women suffer from a 'fear of success'. The evidence of this chapter is that diagnoses of reticence mask systemic obstacles as personal failings. Prevalent ways of interpreting women's reticence about leadership—as fear of success and faltering commitment, an unsuitability/illfittedness for leadership—need to be understood as another means of preserving the ideology of leadership, safe from challenge or change.

Women are nervous about putting themselves into the category of leadership for several good reasons which have little to do with their ability or even confidence. Their apparent reticence stems from their understanding of the construct of leadership, from their experience that others often don't judge what they do as being leadership and from a tendency to under-estimate rather than over-estimate their value to the organisation.

Firstly, many women see leadership in partially negative terms, as requiring an ambition, single-mindedness or ruthlessness which may be all right for others but not for themselves. For women, leadership is not the 'motherhood' value which it is for many men. You won't find them enthusiastically extolling the need for leadership visions to the same extent as men, and they are more likely to envisage the dark sides and the qualifications to strong leadership. Why is this so? I have argued elsewhere that, because leaders tend to be male, leadership is facilitated by a process of projective identification; that is, followers see in male leaders aspects of the men they would like to be. This process, though it can occur with women, is more muted—not so vivid and direct.

Secondly, the critical audiences who judge one's eligibility for leadership (they are typically male) often fail to recognise the activities of women—in persuading, judging, directing, controlling—as leadership. Finally, as research also supports, women tend to undervalue their performance and contribution, so they may be slow to see what they do as qualifying as leadership.

These effects are often combined with the dynamics of tokenism for women in senior roles. The work of Kanter (1977) in particular has shown how difference leads to a range of other experiences such as tokenism, high visibility and isolation. The dynamics of tokenism include a tendency for others to disregard performance, instead focusing on aspects of difference or womanliness. They tend to evaluate this woman against ideal standards of what women should do or be. Visiblity and isolation are simultaneously exaggerated. At the same time, the entrance of a token to a group has the effect of making formerly disparate group members more cohesive. The dominant group displays discomfort, then exaggerates norms and interests which unite them and exclude the token.

Some observers have taken women's circumspection about leading as evidence of inadequacy for leadership roles. A preference for consultation has been judged as indecisiveness, expressions of doubt as the mark of insufficient toughness. Others have drawn simplistic and essentialist conclusions that all women lead 'differently'. The evidence presented in this chapter underlines the need to avoid simplistic conclusions but also to recognise the lack of connection many women feel with conventional understandings of leadership. We need to broaden the category of leadership so that it can encapsulate and symbolise the work that many of these women are already doing.

7

STRATEGIES USED BY WOMEN TO INFLUENCE

How do women in authority seek to influence others? I have shown how women encounter particular obstacles as they acquire power in organisations, obstacles which have to do with their gender rather than, for example, style of leading. Just as women encounter distinctive obstacles, there are distinctive strategies women use to influence others and gain power. I argue in this chapter that women build and assert authority in the context of the constraints described, while at the same time modelling particular priorities and concerns, and so interweaving their womanliness into their leadership roles.

Much has been written on power and influence in executive roles. The widely accepted contemporary view is that the wise and responsible use of power is essential for a senior executive. According to Kotter (1986) this is because of the 'power gap'; that is, one's formal authority rarely amounts to enough influence to achieve desired organisational outcomes—position power needs to be supplemented by other sources of influence. Similarly, in most categorisations of bases of power, formal authority—also understood as legitimate or position power—is regarded as an insufficient basis on which to build leadership.

Other bases of power and influence on which executives have traditionally drawn include network power, centrality, information power, intelligence, expertise, power to reward or coerce and, last but not least, personal power. Personal power is generally seen to derive from a range of characteristics including charisma, reputation, judgement, toughness (Pfeffer 1992), confidence, endurance and physical stamina. Summarising research, Dainty and Anderson conclude that gender, physical attributes (sexuality/size) and personality/charm make up the ingredients of personal power, and they refer to a poll of American CEOs in which personality was 'ranked amongst the three most important powerbases' (1996: 102).

Personal characteristics can thus contribute to, or undermine, one's power base and available repertoires of influence strategies. Gender and physical attributes such as height and stature are particularly palpable ingredients of power (one study of American political leaders found they were more than likely to be tall, first-born sons). Male physical characteristics are more likely to be associated in an organisational context with power; even before they open their mouths or act, men are more likely to be endowed with power and the potential for leadership.

In the assessment of qualities such as 'stamina', 'confidence' and 'toughness', it is highly unlikely that definitions are gender-neutral. Indeed the argument made throughout this book is that leadership in practice has been defined by the implicit presence of masculinity. It is (male) stamina, (male) confidence and (male) toughness that is being looked for, and endorsed, as evidence of leadership.

The success and range of influence strategies used depends on how the user is perceived—on perceptions of personal power and other characteristics. Strategies such as 'authority', 'bargaining', 'reason/logic', 'friendliness' and the capacity to enforce 'sanctions' are more likely to be available and effective when they are paired with salient sources of personal power, such as confidence, reputation, toughness.

So, when women think about influencing, their capacity to draw on traditional strategies can be limited. For example, before they can bargain effectively, women may need to overcome pre-existing stereotypes of their lacking toughness; before they draw on friendly persuasion to influence, they may need to dispense with other stereotyped misreadings of their motives.

Turning to the question of whether men and women exhibit different influence styles, or are differently effective in influencing, findings from empirical studies offer a complex picture (for a recent review, see Watson and Hoffman 1996). Broadly, research postulates, and finds, a tendency for women to adopt more collaborative and less competitive strategies for influencing, to be consultative and focus on organisational outcomes rather than self-interest (Lauterbach and Weiner 1996).

However, a number of factors mitigate firm conclusions. First is a methodological problem about how influence strategies are tested. Laboratory studies of leadership and influence strategies are notoriously limited, often engaging 'participants in a task of no consequence to them' (Berdahl 1996). In observational as opposed to laboratory studies of leading men and women, it is argued that by the time women achieve positions of formal power, they have learned and share similar influencing strategies to their male colleagues: they have become enculturated. And the scarcity of women in such leadership roles means that sample sizes are inevitably very small and that extrapolation to a wider population should always be cautious.

The difficulty of separating the effects of gender from power is another significant limitation on research findings. In her study of a large bureaucracy and in further research, Kanter (1977; 1979) concludes that influence behaviours are determined less by gender than by power. Overlapping effects can be explained by the fact that in most organisations those with significant power are also men.

The effects of gender on negotiation and upward influence tactics are examined in two recent studies (Watson and Hoffman 1996; Xin and Tsui 1996). Both find no significant gender differences. However, Xin and Tsui draw our attention to the special effects that come into play at the top of organisations, where 'effectiveness becomes defined by social criteria as differences in competency narrow'. Thus:

> Managers whose styles match those of superiors may benefit from the 'similar to me' effect in performance evaluations and promotion decisions. Managers whose styles differ from those of superiors may not accrue the same rewards and recognition even though they may be equally effective in getting things done (Lauterbach and Weiner 1996: 104).

Studies of women leading entrepreneurial ventures overcome some of these methodological issues, since such organisational environments give women greater opportunity to lead in a way that suits them. Indeed, one of the reasons why women are said to leave large organisations is that they have little choice but to conform to a well-established model of leadership. In her study of over five hundred women-led organisations in New Zealand, Judith Pringle (1996) found that when women are able to choose, they tend to run their organisations in a more open, consultative and less hierarchical manner than is found in many male-led organisations.

To sum up, much of the theory and research on power and influence in organisations has been gender-blind. Studies have been largely based on observations of men in authority, and conclusions about effective power and influence have been extrapolated to the general population of managers. It might be argued that this has arisen simply because the population of observable leaders has been overwhelmingly male, and that our task is now to chart more systematically the way leading women influence in a broader range of settings than just the male-dominated corporation.

The 'add women and stir' approach, as this way of making research more gender-inclusive is sometimes known (Sinclair 1995d), would remedy some of the deficiencies of leadership research. However, recognition is also needed of the way in which models of influence and negotiation tactics have been developed and constructed around the assumption of a male leader. In practice, this often means that women are tested against an implicitly male norm, that discernible differences are observed and the conclusion drawn that women are deficient.

These findings about research on influence and gender highlight my more general argument about the need to reveal how gender and leadership are constructed in organisational contexts. Built into organisational cultures are norms about what constitutes 'effective' influence strategies. The same strategies, when employed by men and women will, because of broader societal and cultural norms, be judged differentially appropriate and effective. For example, openly adversarial or combative tactics when exhibited in some organisational contexts by men will be seen as indicative of focus and 'well-directed aggression'. But in an example from my research, one woman's loud laughing and assertive physical gesture of throwing her head back while part of a lunch-time group was judged by a male CEO as inappropriate and evidence of 'trying to be too like the boys'. Similarly, rough locker-room language including swearing is generally viewed as acceptable when used by men, among largely male groups. It may be read as showing the seriousness of a situation, and among men is a vehicle for expressing strong emotions which might otherwise be taboo. The same language used by a woman in authority is judged as utterly inappropriate, even shocking, and it undermines rather than strengthens her claim to be taken seriously.

A further weakness in much of the organisational research on power is that it tends to take a person-centred and individualistic perspective. An alternative understanding of power recognises that it is systemic, often invisibly and impalpably exercised, without a clear victim and without a perpetrator (Lukes 1974). Power can be present but people subject to it may be unaware of its exercise.

These weaknesses in analyses warn us against over-simplified accounts of women enjoying freedom of choice in the way they build power and exercise influence. To grasp the range of influence strategies exhibited and preferred by women we need to understand the traditionally male cultures in which women often operate and the role of women's conscious and unconscious knowledge about 'what works'. The women I interviewed rely on distinctive influence strategies, especially non-confrontational ones, and it is to these that I now turn.

The influence strategies used by the women are listed in Table 2, and I will discuss each of them. I include those that were mentioned by at least half the sample, either as part of their own repertoire or as part of the style of leading women they admire. The list should not be regarded as comprehensive or treated as strategies exclusive to women. However, many of them have been identified in other research of senior women. For example, Marshall documents similar strategies and preferences in influencing among her interviewees, for example, 'relational styles of management' and 'professionalism and effectiveness' (1995a).

TABLE 2: INFLUENCE STRATEGIES USED BY LEADING WOMEN

Directed Upward and Across (to superiors, peers and clients)

Focus on Making a Contribution
- emphasis on contribution to industry, field or profession
- relish in the intellectual challenge
- outcomes emphasis or problem-solving focus

Submerging Ego
- giving others opportunities to make key decisions
- being prepared for others to look better than oneself to produce a desired outcome
- being prepared to be stereotyped as, for example, overly cautious or withholding to produce a good outcome
- 'taking a back seat'

Being a Confidante
- being a safe and trusted ally
- being mentored: to metaphorically 'sit at the knee' of a mentor, be guided and learn
- being a good listener
- avoiding rivalry and being seen as a competitor
- actively downplaying one's aspirations

Persistence and Professionalism
- never being seen to give up
- resolute impartiality and, on occasion, emphasised gender-neutrality

Surprise, Shock and Challenge

Seeking Advice and Creating a Network
- from trusted advisors and consultants
- building contacts beyond the organisation, e.g. in the wider industry or with other women.

TABLE 2 *contd*

Directed Downward (to subordinates)
Building a Team
* strategic appointments of other women
* helping others 'be their best'

Defined Boundaries
* limiting social interaction with subordinates
* not leaving oneself open to allegations of favouritism
* being in control in the case of sexual attraction or overtures

Avoiding 'Slanging Matches'
* calmness, avoiding outbursts and being cornered
* use of departure and distance

Focus on Making A Contribution

Leadership, for most of the women in my research, was not in itself a prize. In fact, for reasons discussed in the preceding chapter, many women feel ambivalent about having the top job. When combined with a tendency to underplay rather than overstate their contribution, it is not surprising that being appointed a leader is not something from which women derive a simple and straightforward sense of satisfaction. Because of their own ambivalence, and that of those with whom they work and depend, women often focus on the wider contribution they make to an industry or field; the sense of satisfaction in the intellectual challenge or in solving a particular long-standing problem. Thinking of a very successful female peer, one woman gave this description:

> She sort of takes it as it comes provided she gets an intellectual reward and stimulus out of it. I don't think in her mind's eye she sees herself as chairman of a bank or a major corporation. She would rather address the challenges that each particular circumstance presents to her, master it and then move on.

Focusing on an overarching professional or industry contribution is a critical psychological safety-net for many women who, at different stages of their career, have experienced rejection and even ridicule from peers. Linda describes this process as 'creating new definitions of winning'. It means that if one suffers significant career or organisational setbacks, there is still a well-developed understanding of how one has made a difference, and will continue to do so. One woman who runs her own business maintains:

> I do whatever I can to stay in business, because being in business gives me a place in the industry and gives me a certain position of power even though I am perhaps derided or neglected or whatever, but in my own eyes I have that position and that influence and that power.

This woman seeks to consolidate her contribution by writing articles for a professional magazine and speaking at conferences. Other interviewees realised their contribution through leadership of professional or women's groups. In many cases, contribution could be more securely established beyond the immediate confines of their organisation. Creating a profile and establishing contribution outside the organisation is also a sensible career strategy if the organisational climate becomes hostile.

Submerging Ego

According to one interviewee, women 'are not prepared to go into a huge war'. This tendency not to be so driven by the need for personal status and recognition has some costs for women who are reluctant to blow their own trumpet. It is recognised that 'it is hard to do, to talk about your own successes'. Among a group of women chief executives, 'almost the more senior they are and the more responsibility they shoulder, they are genuinely quiet about it and just accept they have done that . . . they will just talk about it very quietly and be able to express very well where they want to be'. Other women who don't conform to this ethos of humility are sometimes judged as being inexperienced or immature.

One woman describes the challenge of submerging ego in a negotiation: 'sitting in a meeting with an external group where you are trying to negotiate an agreement where you both want something . . . feeling furious because they're just being bloody minded'. Her approach is not to 'push your way through' but to seek common ground: 'try and give them something of what they want':

I can see what they mean and you know, maybe it is important to give them what they need as much as it is to give me what I think I need. So it disarms me, makes me think about what it is we should be trying to win. I mean, it means winning isn't what I thought it was, winning will change in its nature.

Drawing on empathy doesn't mean that women aren't capable of being fiercely determined and competitive. It may mean, however, that female leaders focus their competitive urges more upon those outside the organisation. Submerging ego and using empathy can then create new opportunities: 'I find that every time I can sort of see it from their point of view, I make partnerships more than try and compete and knock them off'. And they also seek to balance the single-mindedness of playing it tough with affirmation of the value of an underlying relationship. One CEO told the story of another female leader locked in a legal battle: 'As soon as she won the case, she went and gave the guy a gift and started to re-open relationships with him again'.

When dealing with her boss, the head of the firm, Elizabeth's tactics involve thinking ahead, using different strategies for different kinds of decisions, and having contingency plans. Her overriding concern is to get the outcome she seeks, and she subjugates personals needs for recognition or glory to this end:

. . . his first reaction to anything you say to him is to take the op-posite position. But I don't have a problem with that. To me that is just part of a congenital need that he has to make sure we have thought of everything . . . There is kind of two ways I can tackle it. One is to go in and say, well here is the decision and here is my rec-ommendation and then typically he will say 'Well shouldn't we do the reverse and here are all the reasons why'. And I will often set it up that way. So I can then say 'I see exactly where you're coming from. I have already thought about it and here are all the reasons why you're wrong . . . Alternatively, I will put it to him in the posi-tive, this is typically for the bigger decisions. I will make a strong recommendation and I will actually set out exactly why and the thought processes I have gone through.

Part of the strategy of submerging ego involves a preparedness to 'take a back seat' for while—to listen, observe and learn 'how it all works'. This is a difficult and delicate balance which female directors who join formerly all-male Boards also describe. It is important 'not to jump in' prematurely, but it is also important for one's confidence to make a useful contribution not too far into one's tenure. The problem is particularly notable for women because of their visibility. For reasons outlined elsewhere in the book, the first and only woman on a Board is watched more closely than her male colleagues. The value of what she says also stands for future and potential women.

In general, the women interviewees deal with their visibility through 'doing their homework' (being well prepared and well briefed), and through adept interpersonal skills (understanding underlying dynamics and choosing the timing and topic of their contributions).

Being a Confidante

Whether running their own business or working at a senior level in large organisations, women place great stress on the need to build trust, to be a good listener and, if necessary, to downplay one's own ambitions. Becoming a confidante confers two-way benefits. Nora describes how this has worked in her relationships with a couple of long-standing male mentors, former chief executives in the industry to which she was consulting:

> In my industry we go to a lot of functions and you meet people. That is the best way of networking . . . So I had no hesitation about ringing them up and asking, you can always ask. I play that role after many years in my own business. I play that role for other people who want to know something . . . asking me to do something, or do I know such and such . . . If I don't I'll refer them to someone I am sure will be able to tell them. [Why do you think these particular men took an interest in you?] I was, I was like the daughter they never had who was vitally interested in what they did.

Other women find they can establish, over time, very strong relations with clients:

. . . one has to be a personal confidante, one has to be a sounding board, an attentive listener, a good listener. One has to probe below. And women are very good at that.

Katherine describes the development of a close relationship as part of business-building:

. . . there is one particular client, I am sort of semi-matrimonial advisor as well as on a business level . . . the priorities of the business are very much tied to the idionsyncracies of the owner, so you need to understand, you know, what is important to them and their family and what sort of drives them.

As described in *Trials at the Top*, men who lead often feel both lonely and isolated. There is sometimes intense rivalry within senior management teams and taboos against leaders sharing their doubts or asking for help. Some interviewees find that being a woman is an asset in establishing rapport and trust with a client, boss, peer or Board member: 'there is not that competitive spirit there is when he is dealing with a male':

. . . they often haven't got anyone to talk to. It is so closed and then when they have an opportunity to talk to someone that is safe, even though you might be equal in power, you are not really because you are a woman . . . so therefore you are not a threat. So a lot of men (I work with) talk about their lives, lives of quiet desperation and how they hate all the games . . .

Building closer relationships and being open also adds to the satisfaction of the job: 'I think if you like people and are comfortable dealing with them, you put more of your heart and soul into it.'

Persistence and Professionalism

In their dealings with superiors within their organisation and with clients, women rely on persistence and professionalism as the means to win through. Doggedness, hard work and a track record are the underpinnings of this kind of influence, the less glamorous alternatives to charisma. Sometimes these are consciously chosen substitutes for the high degree of competitiveness and toughness which women see in male peers, and feel they can't, or don't want to, emulate. Nora, for example, remarks:

> I am not tough but I am persistent, very persistent. I am very even tempered, I don't lose my cool . . . [How do you deal with failures and setbacks?] Well, we had one major stuff-up probably once a year in the firm . . . And so I ring the client and say we have stuffed it, may we try again please. And that is how to deal with failure—we have stuffed it, let's do it again.

Another accepts that, in a new chief executive role, long hours are inevitable: 'I work extraordinary hours . . . at the moment I can't do my job properly the way I want to do it, because I spend my day with people, spend the day at meetings and all of the paperwork has to be done at night'.

Surprise, Shock and Challenge

Women sometimes actively draw on their difference to surprise people, to say the unsayable or take a dissenting view. Several interviewees expressed pleasure in selectively deflating the 'self-righteousness', 'self-importance' and 'stuffiness' of senior people they work with.

Particularly for women working in advisory or internal consulting roles to executive teams, a frequent strategy involves being courageous and naming what is going on:

> I enjoy being in a position where I can challenge and confront [Why do you like it?] I think it is stimulating . . . um . . . I mean I enjoy provocation . . . basically say to people 'I don't think you are serious about changing anything, in fact I think you are all dead from the neck down.'

Such influence tactics are generally more sustainable when one is an external adviser, although in a few cases women's organisational reputations are built on being forthright, not trapped in the obsequiousness that can pervade senior teams. This, of course, can also be a lonely and risky path.

Women are accustomed to being sex-stereotyped and are adept at using the complacency of others' comfortable categorisations to achieve particular ends. Said one: 'I am the unthreatening motherly type, so I can say things'. Another talked about understanding the categories into which women are typically slotted by the men in her organisation: 'nurturing mother', 'daughter', 'super-bitch', 'lover . . . someone that has slept their way to the top . . . or you are a lesbian'. Sandy actively uses surprise to resist categorisation: 'because they can't box you and because all these other ones are discounted then it actually makes you more influential'.

Seeking Advice and Creating a Network

Many of the interviewees are open about seeking the advice of mentors or friends outside their organisation, as well as obtaining paid consulting advice to assist in aspects of the leadership task. One argues that many of the male networks she encounters are highly self-protective. This extends from social through to employing arrangements: 'once they've employed someone it's very difficult for them to say I've made a mistake':

> I have decided that there are horses for courses and some people are more skilled in some areas. And therefore unlike many men, I take advice . . . you know I keep saying 'Well, what happened there?' and use it as a training ground. But many men wouldn't admit that.

Building a Team

According to some research, women leaders prefer to influence their subordinates by consultative rather than directive or coercive means (Rosener 1990; Helgesen 1990; Pringle 1996). There was evidence for this preference among the emphases of my interviewees. They choose staff very carefully and seek to get good organisational outcomes by bringing out the best in others, described by one interviewee as 'getting people to work out their own visions and not just fulfill mine'. Achieving 'balance' in a team, making sure the men and the women in the team are those who are more comfortable working with a female boss, and selecting people who complement one's own strengths were all frequently mentioned: 'I have never been frightened to do that—to try and get people who are better than me underneath me, to support me'.

These female bosses take particular things into account, in addition to the formal job requisites, when recruiting male team members. When selecting men, women find that a high degree of ambition is a concern. Instead they will often seek out men who are older, perhaps closer to retirement or more comfortable with their career and with less to prove. Younger men who are experienced and enjoy working with women, or who for well-understood personal reasons have resolved to work according to different values, are also preferred.

Women who are in a position to hire employees also gain considerable satisfaction from supporting the careers of more junior women, recruiting women with less traditional career paths into their organisation and advocating for recognition of other women's (under-valued) potential.

As with a number of women, it took Katherine a while before she felt confident enough to mentor younger women in her organisation. Some senior women do not feel secure enough about their own position to risk strong support for other women in the organisation. Advocacy for other women is construed by some male peers as reverse discrimination (though the same men practise long-standing habits of patronage themselves), and women find that their credibility is too damaged by this process. Katherine summarises the tensions felt by senior women in her mentoring of a capable but out-spoken younger woman, also highlighting the conflicts of style discussed in the preceding chapter:

> If it's the last thing I do in that office, I want to see her get up. But I have got to be careful because the more I champion the cause, the more I put some of the others off. So its going to need some very careful handling . . . She isn't ready, but I think she will be in twelve months time, but she still doesn't have the across-the-board support she needs . . . Some are saying, are querying whether she will ever be the right person. I think she is, she just needs a little maturing . . . And she has been a bit of a stirrer, I mean she has needed to mature. She has been quite good, but she really is quite blunt and just sort of issues of tact—you don't make a complete fool of one of your employers in front of your most junior staff.

Working to support other women is something that gives some senior women great satisfaction. However, one suspects it must sometimes be accomplished with higher standards of professionalism than apply to the intra-organisational networking of men. The spectre of women working together attracts theories of conspiracy, while traditions of men doing so, such as sharing a game of golf or going to the football, are regarded as the normal workings of business.

The evidence is that women pay attention to, and derive satisfaction from, building the contributions of others. There are occasions, however, when strong direction is required. The expectation, even stereotype, that women consult can create difficulties in those circumstances:

> . . . women are very vulnerable because we are really under scrutiny. People do look at us differently. First of all, I think women expect us to manage differently and are disappointed when we don't fit that absolute consensus model.

Defined Boundaries

Negotiation of professional–private boundaries is particularly complicated for senior women. As discussed in Chapter 2, women are expected to be more interested in one's family, health and welfare, and to be more understanding when personal crises occur. This means that women are often required to define the limits of their understanding, while their male colleagues work within more readily tried and tested boundaries. Female leaders also find that they may be regarded as threatening by male colleagues' partners. This is another reason why women sometimes feel the need to work harder to maintain, and be seen to maintain, a 'professional distance' from colleagues and subordinates.

The need for boundaries between one's professional and personal lives takes different forms at different career stages. At early stages of careers, establishing clear boundaries and formal distance from male colleagues can be essential to avoid the innuendo and sexualisation that accompany women when they enter male cultures: 'No-one could come near me. I was very nice, very pleasant, but there was a very strong boundary'.

As they become senior, or if they move into the position of CEO, women often find the need to re-draw boundaries. These can include substituting more professional relations for friendly and informal relationships. Because it is harder for women to be experienced as both an authoritative boss and an approachable friendly one, many women find they need to create more distance from subordinates and adopt more formal standards of interaction than men in their position might. Women constantly draw on their empathy and friendships at work. However, sometimes this can be misconstrued by subordinates who see it as an invitation for special consideration and by others who regard it as a form of favouritism. As they take on leadership positions, some women stopped socialising with more junior colleagues, or were more careful about the invitations they accepted and the aspects of private lives they shared with or divulged to colleagues.

These strategies of maintaining clear professional boundaries condemned some women to more formality and solitariness than they would otherwise have sought. Although male leaders also experience this, I have argued that it is a greater challenge for women because they are expected to be friendly and interested in subordinates' personal lives and because they often prefer relationships that are warm and empathic. One CEO talks of her rather reluctant decision not to return dinner-party invitations. Others talk about rationing 'out of hours' contact with subordinates.

The pressures leave women in a position of constructed invulnerability, where it can be hard to share jokes, failures or doubts. Sandy admits: 'it's a very isolating job'. She routinely leaves dinners and functions early and is always restrained in what she drinks and says, because of the high visibility she knows she has. And the active and continual management of boundaries adds an extra dimension to her job: 'You are the one who has to manage it. I have to manage all this stuff as well [as the job at hand] and you have to be very clear about it, otherwise you are the one who can end up being very vulnerable'.

Once defined, however, having clear boundaries can be liberating for both the women themselves and the people who work with and for them. The point is that, in the case of women, these often need to be more explicitly and carefully negotiated, defended and maintained. This imposes a personal cost for women who, as described in Chapter 9, often settle for greater distance than they would choose. This path can also condemn women to greater loneliness and isolation in their role as leader than many men experience.

Avoiding 'Slanging Matches'

As one of the two most senior executives in Australia who can give corporate approval for significant financial transactions, Elizabeth describes in this extended quote how she exercises this level of power and how she deals with the occasional situation of more junior men bringing pressure to bear:

> I am typically confronted with situations where people need me to approve what they are doing . . . I work very hard at sort of not, you know, sitting with my arms crossed and frowning at people, but that is often dynamics that's going on—it is people trying to convince me that what they want to do is a good idea. And 90 per cent of the time, in fact, what they are proposing is perfectly fine and un-contentious . . . it is relatively unusual to get a full on, face to face, shouting match with someone—although in the last couple of months I have had about three of these and that has been a real learning experience for me because that is *very unusual* to have an *open hostility in this firm* . . . if it is a big decision that is a bit contentious, I need to keep [the other senior executive] involved and the circumstances I am thinking of recently where we had the slanging matches, he was involved all along . . . It was kind of interesting to me because at no time did anyone question the validity of my having the view I had. In this business, there is no right answer to a lot of the questions we have to tackle . . . part of the process was making sure that my [internal] client was educated about the change in my view [a changed assessment of risk on a proposed deal] and overcoming a feeling on their part that I was being capricious or inconsistent. So we kind of worked it all through . . . That wasn't too bad. When we really came to *blows* was when they came back two weeks later and said that deal never happened . . . that was when there was this nuclear explosion [laughs] French

testing, absolute nuclear explosion. This was a conversation that took place at ten past six on a Friday night when I had dinner guests [laughs] . . . it was pretty ugly and the individual involved, in fact, I've sat next to him before and I had seen him in action before and I didn't take any of the explosion particularly personally. But it nonetheless had to be dealt with and he was striding around the office calling me names and shouting at the top of his voice. We have an open office plan, so, I mean, like the *whole office* heard it . . .

[How did you deal with that?] I guess some people sort of get very much back in the other person's face. I tend to pull back and to kind of shut down. And I basically said 'Well, I am going to go and sit back down at my desk. When you are ready to talk about this, come and talk about it'. At which point he simmered down some- what, sort of came around to my work area and did ultimately sit down, which to me was very significant body language . . . I am not prepared to engage in that sort of conversation because that is just not people trying to come to a meeting of minds . . . And we did ultimately get there [agree on the deal].

Elizabeth uses a range of strategies to ground herself and strengthen her position without behaving autocratically or getting involved in 'slanging matches'. She tries to be approachable, not automatically adopting a 'No, till you can change my mind' position. She makes sure she has the support of senior colleagues if a decision is likely to be contentious, and she reassures herself that there aren't any right answers. Elizabeth stores away the evidence that no-one questioned the 'validity' of her taking a different view. In the confrontation, she gains control of the situation by refusing to be provoked, using a 'cooling off' period for both parties to regain com- posure, and reconvening where she can assert her authority more confidently—at her desk rather than in public space.

The Derivation of Women's Influence Strategies

My research indicates that senior women draw on a distinctively dif- ferent repertoire of strategies and tactics to influence than those identified from studies comprising men. Gender is an essential variable in understanding the range of strategies available to, and effectively used by, senior executives. Where do women's strategies come from?

I want to suggest that there are two sets of factors at work here. The first has to do with how women choose to influence—their values and strengths; the second has to do with the particular difficulties women face in leadership—they have learned that strategies developed and designed for male influence are often less effective when practised by women, so they have adapted and refined alternatives.

In work comparing the play of girls and boys and the consequent development of moral thinking, Carol Gilligan (1977; 1982; 1988) argued that, in general, women exhibit a desire to preserve relationships and minimise hurt, while men place a higher value on observing universal principles of justice and fairness. Gilligan's work has prompted both controversy and attempts to prove the existence of fundamental differences between men and women—in management research as elsewhere. In Chapter 1, I looked at why this debate about the existence of difference focuses on the wrong issues.

However, we should also acknowledge that a range of educational, leadership and other research (for example Belenky *et al.* 1986; Helgesen 1990; Rosener 1990) finds that, if they perceive they have a choice, women will tend to opt for consultative styles of influence, giving a high priority to communicating and to building and maintaining relationships.

Speculating on this troublesome question, one of my interviewees volunteered: 'I don't think because I'm a woman means I'm more empathic than other people'. While wary about such differences being construed as uniquely feminine or maternal qualities, in her case she considers the origins of it may lie in her mothering:

> . . . your heart does break for your child . . . there is something about having experienced that when you've got little kids, about just *lurching*, your heart *lurching* as they have to do things.

She repeats that this habit of putting yourself in another's shoes, feeling with and for others, is not exclusive to women or to women with children. But she does regard it as a process that women tend to use to effect better organisational outcomes than a more competitive process might achieve. In a sense this is the 'win–win' negotiating strategy often recommended to managers, but embedded in the more female language of empathy.

The context in which women operate and the fact that female leaders are typically perceived differently to men constitutes the second set of factors which, I argue, have shaped how they influence. In earlier chapters I have speculated that women with power often act as magnets for unresolved anxieties and dependencies—for both men and women. At a deep and typically unconscious level, powerful women evoke ambivalent feelings about mothers and women in general. And many of the dilemmas and pressures described by the women interviewed provide examples of these feelings at work. One woman alludes to this specifically:

> . . . men and women in the workplace headed by a woman invariably see women in more of a parent role . . . Sometimes this stimulates really hard stuff and I don't think all men or all women can, in this current culture of our generation, bear to work for a woman. I mean if their mother's stuff is so unworked through . . .

That women continue to be judged as mothers as well as leaders is evident in expectations of consensus-building leadership, of bottomless understanding of personal crises. Several interviewees mentioned the difficulties of attracting the envy of other women, of subordinates 'consumed with envy'. Others described the desire of male subordinates to outdo female leaders, driven by a deep need to prove their mastery, and masculinity.

Women who have been strong role models for other women sometimes become exhausted by the extra visibility and workload. Leading women are not only expected to do their job, but to do it in a way which supports and empowers other women. Many women have been appointed to Boards and senior levels of organisations with this task as an unwritten additional part of their job description. After a long period working directly and indirectly on women's issues, one interviewee craved the anonymity of just being a senior executive: 'I've had enough of being the woman's woman'.

These extra pressures—to be 'a good mother' as well as leader; to empower others and put one's own ambitions on hold; to advocate for all women—undoubtedly shape the complexity of influence strategies described by interviewees. The need to re-define personal–professional boundaries a little more rigidly partially reflects a need to minimise the maternalisation of women's authority. Focusing on a broader contribution enables women to develop careers along simultaneous pathways. If they encounter organisational resistance, for example, they have alternative avenues along which to pursue aspirations. Identity and self-esteem are not totally tied to organisational approval.

Women may well prove, in a comprehensive analysis of influence strategies, to be bi-gendered in their approach. That is, they learn an array of influence tactics depending on the context, who they are working with, how much power they have and whether influencing upwards or downwards. Berdahl (1996) finds that while most men primarily operate in one male-dominated and individualistic organisational culture, women typically move across several subcultures. Women become attuned to the norms and adapt to the prevalent strategies of the dominant culture, while staying in touch with their own (sometimes discrepant) preferences for interaction. And they are sensitive to how gender frames the way their actions are judged—for example, as a standard for all women (Kanter 1977).

The importance of sensitivity to local 'currencies' in seeking to influence is pointed out by Dainty and Anderson (1996). In organisations with a traditional male culture, 'thanks' or 'welcome' might be expressed between men in an invitation to join a squash or tennis match. Because they are scarce and new to many organisations, senior women are rarely recipients of these easy, well-understood gestures. Instead they are required to choose their influence strategies more deliberatively. In relying on sanctions or assertiveness to get others to do what they want, mirroring the local currency is likely to prove particularly ineffective. Women, we conclude, need to learn and become adept at using several currencies of influence, and to develop new and additional strategies that reflect the constraints of their context and their own preferences.

About Change

8 CHANGE: *Resistance and Opportunities*

Men and women have, on the whole, very different perceptions of the need for change in gender relations at work. This should surprise no-one. While many women share a strong interest in change, few men share either a perception of the need for change or an interest in it. Although evidence indicates that homosexual men, for example, have more to gain from and are more supportive of arguments for change, traditionally men have supported arguments for patience and time as remedies for residual inequities. This approach is seen by many women as code language for doing nothing, for preserving the status quo.

In this chapter I explore why and how men and women have different views of the need for change. I also dissect the make-up of male resistance—arguments centring on power and interests, and psychological arguments about masculine revulsion for the feminine.

Turning to the question of how change happens, I begin with an overview of the arguments for change based on business logic, including human capital calculations and the globalisation rhetoric and the view that diverse workforces reflect and better serve the reality of a global and diverse marketplace. Such arguments often stay at the level of rhetoric, espoused in mission statements but not necessarily matched in practice. The evidence is that economic arguments alone don't drive change—that managers respond selectively to this evidence, screening out those eloquently argued imperatives which contradict deeper impulses.

Change is more likely to spring from the changing circumstances of people's lives. I look at changes in men's lives: the rigours of the dual-career couple lifestyle; the increased attention to male health and the costs of overwork and stress; the broader men's movement with its emphases on finding space for men to father and the freedom

to express sexualities. Individual households will be the site of reconstructed gender ideas, not only about who has primary care of
children, but about who leads in the workplace.

Why Changes are Resisted

A long-time observer of the effects of sex and gender in organisational life identifies four common explanations for the persisting absence of women from public life and leadership roles: the
individual-deficit model, structural factors, sex-roles and intergroup phenomena (Gutek 1993). I summarise these four common
explanations before examining some underlying reasons for resistance to change: denial and disbelief; 'fear of the feminine' and 'identification with the aggressor'.

The individual-deficit model, also identified as the 'person-
centred' (Riger and Galligan 1980) or 'women-centred' view, sees
the problems residing with individuals, mostly women. Their
'deficits' may be to do with character, training, commitment or
experience, and the remedies offered focus on helping these individuals 'get up to speed'. This argument, as described in Chapter 2, is
often associated with 'the pipeline' assumption and prescribes that,
with time and patience, the pipeline of training and experience will
eventually deliver greater numbers of women who have managed to
compensate for their deficits and to take their place in leadership
roles. The obvious attraction, and shortcoming, of the individual-
deficit argument is that blame is firmly attributed to 'the victim',
who is also expected to fix things: 'it removes responsibility from
organisations and allows the status quo and the power structure to
continue unchallenged' (Gutek 1993: 306).

The structural model, which attributes women's lack of progress
in organisations to the structure of power and opportunity, is the
second of Gutek's explanations. Often cited is Rosabeth Moss
Kanter's *Men and Women of the Corporation* (1977). Kanter's pioneering
work argued that power, not gender, explained organisational
outcomes of sex-segregation, marginalisation and tokenism. She
proposed a form of 'critical mass' argument on the basis of her
research, specifically predicting that organisations composed of

either 'balanced' (50/50 per cent or 60/40 per cent) or 'tilted' (65/35 per cent) distributions of men and women would produce more open and less discriminatory cultures.

The primacy of sex-roles, whereby society defines sex-appropriate behaviours and attitudes to which women and men are captive, is Gutek's third argument. Fourthly, Gutek points to the argument that when groups interact, one will be dominant and the other marginalised and treated as token. This argument is also made from a very different direction by those theorists interested in the construction of difference. According to this view, most notably advanced by the French theorist Derrida, the attribution of difference is never a benign act, but one in which 'difference' is always attributed by those with power to the characteristics of less powerful groups.

Each of these explanations has enjoyed currency at different times and appeals to particular groups. In the present circumstances of market deregulation and withdrawal of government intervention, there is a widespread tendency to individualise both the problem and the solution to discrimination. Lack of individual effort is broadly responsible for problems and outcomes according to this ideology, which also rejects government intervention as a means to remedy discrimination. Change achieved through market-based incentives and rational human-capital arguments are more palatable and favoured.

All these explanations offer instructive insights that by and large have been well-elaborated in research. Here, I want to delve deeper into the psychological reasons for resistance to change in gender relations, examining the bases of denial and disbelief, 'fear of the feminine' and 'identification with the aggressor'.

Denial and Disbelief

There is a saying that identifies two bases of resistance to change in gender relations, typically from men: 'They just don't *get* it'. This phrase highlights, first, that if men don't have the experience of discrimination, then their first reaction is often disbelief. They maintain that it doesn't exist, that women are imagining or at least wildly overstating the discrimination they experience. Second, if men aren't victims of the discriminatory downside of the status quo, then they have little reason or incentive to seek change apart from feelings of empathy with women. So, not only do most men not experience 'a problem'; they are apathetic or actively resistant to changing a state of affairs which, in general terms, reflects and advances their interests.

Evidence of masculine disbelief is widely documented and observable in cases of sexual harassment at work and sexual abuse in family contexts. When studies reveal the incidence of reported harassment, for example, the findings are often publicly questioned. Scientific validity is examined, definitions of harassment scrutinised and the motives of the researchers or study participants cross-examined. Even when harassment is proven, as in the court case described in Chapter 6, it is often regarded as trivial or insignificant by organisation men. In the words of a number of the female participants in this study: 'They can't see [literally and in a broader sense] the problem'.

There is considerable empirical evidence of minority groups rating discrimination at much higher levels than do majority groups in the same organisation. A pioneering study by Alderfer and Smith (1982) found that blacks and whites exhibited opposite perceptions of promotion opportunities in the same organisation. Among blacks, 62 per cent of men and 53 per cent of women said that whites were promoted more rapidly than equivalent blacks. The agreement among whites was only 4 per cent and 7 per cent. When the question was reversed, asking whether blacks enjoyed greater promotion, whites agreed (75 and 82 per cent) much more than blacks (12 and 13 per cent).

In a study of 268 managers and professionals in the United States, Cox (1993) found that only 26 per cent of white men said that race was important or very important in promotion opportunities, and only 31 per cent thought that gender was important or very important. The percentages of white women, non-white men and non-white women were dramatically higher and directly affected by the race and/or gender of the respondent. For example, among the non-white women 76 per cent said race was important or very important in promotion opportunities, and 82 per cent said gender was. Among white women, 62 per cent rated race and 87 per cent rated gender as important or very important in promotion opportunities.

In another study, managers were asked how much change was needed to create an organisation in which all people could achieve their full potential regardless of racial and cultural differences (Cox 1993). Members of minority groups were three to five times more likely to perceive that the change needed was large. Interestingly, in the kind of change seen as necessary, the majority group volunteered much less change needed in 'interpersonal attitudes' than in 'organization culture'. The clear tendency, here as elsewhere, is to project the requirement for change on to less personally confronting objects, such as the culture.

Finally, a study of 457 psychologists and 209 managers found that perceptions of sex discrimination and reactions to discrimination were stronger for women. Although men tended to share the perception that women were more discriminated against, they believed it to be of a much lower level than did women. This study also importantly found substantial negative effects of perceived discrimination on women's attitude to work—decreased self-efficacy, lower feelings of power, more work conflict. However, women with these perceptions also worked more hours, the researchers concluding that 'women who view their workplace as discriminatory feel they can overcome this obstacle by hard work' (Gutek, Cohen and Tsui 1996: 808).

Linking these differential perceptions to obstacles to change, Rene Redwood (1996), Executive Director of the US Glass Ceiling Commission, reported a 1990 survey which found that 73 per cent of male CEOs didn't believe there was a glass ceiling, while 71 per cent of women vice-presidents did. It is not just that persisting gender differences exist in perceived level of discrimination; but as Redwood concluded, 'the underlying cause for the existence of glass ceilings is the perception of many white males that they as a group are losing— losing competitive advantage, losing control and losing opportunity as a direct consequence of inclusion of women and minorities'. The perception that there is no systemic discrimination against women signals an underlying and unowned fear of loss of power and privilege. It justifies maintaining the status quo and resisting change initiatives.

The denial of systemic discrimination by those with power documented in these studies also explains responses to affirmative action programmes and equal employment opportunity initiatives (Cockburn 1991). Such initiatives are often interpreted by men as giving women 'special treatment', without recognising the benefits that accrue to men within existing institutional arrangements. They interpret selection or promotion of women as due to such initiatives and not the merit of the individuals concerned. These perceptual and attribution processes, described by Burton (1991) as part of the 'mobilisation of masculine bias', are often unconscious, if not rarely reviewed in the light of experience or evidence.

Another clear finding from this research is that members of oppressed groups often exhibit more empathy and support for the plight of other discriminated-against groups. For example, women and gay men, or blacks and people of non-English speaking backgrounds, often become allies in male-dominated organisations.

To sum up, many men see no real need to change gender relations in organisations and society. They see no need because they can see no problem—they have not been victims of direct or systemic discrimination themselves—or because they, in various ways and consciously or unconsciously, benefit from the existing régime. Discrimination, particularly when it is indirect or systemic, invisibly confers benefits on those who already have power and privilege, functioning as a 'power multiplier'. It reduces the number of competitors and keeps the 'rules of the game' insulated from challenge and protective of the majority.

I should note here that there are women who also exhibit denial and disbelief about sex discrimination. They typically do so for the same reasons as some male colleagues—they believe they haven't been the victim of discrimination themselves, or they perceive that the existing régime works to their advantage. This response, and the occurrence of what is sometimes described as 'identification with the aggressor' is described below. As with many male colleagues their disbelief about discrimination can be understood as a rational, if highly individualistic, response to personal circumstances, particularly among younger and less senior women who may not have encountered discrimination.

Fear of the Feminine

The formation of gender identities in early childhood is the basis for another set of explanations for men's resistance to change. Nancy Chodorow (1979) first theorised that, for baby boys, among the first task of identity formation was separation from the primary caregiver, usually the mother. Boys establish their identity through being independent and separate from the mother, through an active rejection of feminine qualities of nurturance and dependence. Through this process, masculinity is seen to be established in opposition to femininity. An expression of feminine care or concern is feared as undermining the fragile and emerging construction of masculinity.

Theories of men's 'fear of the feminine' have been used and misused to help explain some men's misogynistic feelings about women, as well as men's discomfort with emotional expressiveness and intimacy. As Norton (1997) explains, however, much of the research examining the playing out of the 'fear of the feminine' is essentialist. It focuses too heavily on the primary psychological interactions between baby and care-giver (often implictly blaming the mother), rather than attending to how later experience and social institutions construct and confirm aspects of these fears.

Norton argues for a different focus and set of theoretical perspectives in explaining why men often find change of gender-relations threatening and difficult. If masculinities are continually being socially constructed and negotiated, and there are few socially available discursive positions which men can comfortably take up, then it is hardly surprising that the prevalent response from men is continuing disbelief and resistance. According to Norton: 'men could only be expected to question the usefulness of aspects of their identity when prevailing constructions relating to their sense of identity [and masculinity] begin to fail them'. Even if they do experience failure, they will be unlikely to 'solve' that failure through resort to a culturally or discursively sanctioned practice, such as declaring their feelings and seeking intimacy, if they have no history or experience of accessing such a practice. Norton concludes:

> It is not implied that there is no room for men to change. However, it is argued that change will come more from men reflecting on and giving up power, and finding new ways to be without power, than it will from simply working through the emotional scars of infancy, or somehow making conscious their potential feminine qualities (1997: 445).

Identification with the Aggressor

When I present research on obstacles women face, individuals will sometimes volunteer the spectre of the 'Queen Bee'—the senior woman who does not mentor more junior women, who seems more 'macho' than all the other men in the senior management team put together. For women, there is a terrible sense of betrayal in perceiving other women's opposition—indeed there is a tendency to portray the opposition of other women as the cruellest and most severe of all.

Are Queen Bees serious obstacles to change? Although they do figure in some women's experiences, evidence suggests that their influence is often overstated. It is perhaps more interesting to speculate on why the Queen Bee phenomenon arouses such passion and interest. Among women there is clearly an expectation of solidarity. When 'stabbed in the back' by a man, we chide ourselves for being so trusting; when a woman does this we are more likely to be deeply disillusioned. The reasons for this differential reaction go back to those early experiences described in Chapter 2—in general, we set for women a higher standard of caring and nurturance and we expect solidarity among women, partially as a response to powerlessness.

The influence of Queen Bees might also be overstated because of their scarcity and consequent visibility. When senior women are bitchy and ruthless they are noticed, and these features become part of the characterisation of all senior women. Kanter (1977) documents this as a common reaction to token women in organisations—one woman's behaviour comes to stand for all and she is judged against an idealised standard of womanliness.

These processes of stereotyping—expecting nurturance and solidarity while over-emphasising ruthlessness—play into the hands of those who believe that women shouldn't occupy senior roles in organisations. It appeals to embedded archetypes of the 'monstrous feminine' (Creed 1993), of women made mad by power—the rampant, cruel queens and witches of fairy-tale whose excesses are only barely held under control by a corporate straitjacket.

The bases of many of these portrayals should be recognised as society's and organisations' discomfort with female authority. Cruel and ruthless powerful women exist, as do men. There is no particular onus on women to be unilaterally selfless and supportive of other women, just as men don't labour under this extra burden, although research indicates that women's leadership style tends to favour devolved and interactive structures (Pringle 1996).

Some women, then, feel comfortable working with men, perceive no discrimination against them and argue against equal opportunity provisions. This can be a rational reaction to personal experience, either of not encountering discrimination oneself, or of being marginalised as someone who has earned their position from equal opportunity initiatives. The backlash against such programmes affects women by making them resentful because they are prevented from demonstrating or having their true contribution recognised.

Other women, for various reasons often to do with early experiences in life, simply feel more comfortable with men than women. They may have had a strong, or blocked, attachment to fathers or brothers, or they may have felt unconnected to or abandoned by women. Whatever the origins of this male-identification, these women enjoy the company of men, share interests and aspirations that are typically characterised as masculine, and perhaps seek their approval.

In extreme cases this male identification can take the form of 'identification with the aggressor'. This is a construct developed in psychoanalysis to explain how some people, and particularly children, deal with a sense of perceived threat and aggression. According to Anna Freud, 'by impersonating the aggressor, assuming his attributes or imitating his aggression, the child transforms himself into the person who makes the threat' (1961: 121). The identification also enables the child to move from a passive to an active position. Identification with the aggressor has also been used to explain, for example in prisoner-of-war camps and in domestic violence, how victims deal with expectations of aggression towards them and feelings of powerlessness by taking on the characteristics and behaviours of the aggressor. These aggressive behaviours are often then turned not on the original aggressor but on others who are weak or vulnerable.

Although these are extreme situations and it is inappropriate to extrapolate to most corporate settings, identification with the aggressor helps makes sense of some responses to a sense of extreme isolation and powerlessness. If senior women feel victims of covert aggression in a combative environment, it is unsurprising that one unconscious path might be through believing in, and perhaps replicating, the logic and actions of the dominant group. Competitive and adversarial cultures put a premium on power, and subscribing to the rules and norms of such régimes affords a small amount of power, which is better than none. Neither is it surprising that the victims of such ruthless treatment might be other, more junior, women in the organisation.

The conclusion to draw from this analysis is that not all women share a commitment to dismantle discrimination. A range of factors, originating in personal experience and in social conditions of powerlessness, explain why a minority of women passively and actively resist change in gender relations in organisations. It is important to recognise heterogeneity in women's experiences and to understand the bases of feminine opposition to change programmes such as affirmative action. However, the extent of this opposition should not be overstated as this colludes with destructive archetypes of 'monstrous femininity' and limits the notions of leadership we are seeking to change.

The Business Argument

Within economic discourse, discrimination constitutes an irrational managerial practice. In an ideal marketplace, individuals would be selected and rewarded on the basis of their objectively assessed potential and performance. Discrimination in favour of certain groups and against others would rarely occur because of the costs of not choosing optimally from the complete pool of available human capital.

The 'business case' for managing diversity builds on this fundamental logic, arguing that discrimination costs and that effective use of diversity pays (see, for example, Cox and Blake 1991; Morrison 1992; Thomas 1996). Cox and Blake, for example, include the following as reasons for organisations to make good use of their workforce diversity: the cost argument; the resource-acquisition argument (the benefits of a reputation as preferred employer); the marketing argument; the creativity argument; the problem-solving argument, and the system flexibility argument.

A drawback of the bulk of the diversity management research is that it draws on the experiences of American corporations, which have far more significant and well-publicised legal sanctions against discrimination. In the United States, a company's bottom line can be significantly affected by a discrimination action, with pay-outs to claimants of millions of dollars. Companies with 'high quality affirmative action programs . . . contribute to sustaining a competitive advantage and are valued in the marketplace' according to researchers (Wright *et al.* 1995: 283). Within this legal climate, there is a clear economic incentive to manage, or be seen to manage, diversity well.

The Australian context provides a very different set of sanctions against discrimination and incentives to manage diversity. We are less enthusiastic litigators, the fines are smaller and draw less media attention, with the result that both management and shareholders are less likely to see discrimination as a barometer of poor corporate performance. Australian companies have also not had the experience of coming to terms with racial differences. And recent Australian efforts to negotiate with indigenous land-holders suggests that business skills in understanding and working with different racial value systems are under-developed.

The case for managing diversity in the Australian context typically hinges on three sets of incentives to do with employees, customers and markets, and innovation and effectiveness (see Table 3). The employee argument poses that companies which are not appointing, promoting and retaining women among their employees are not utilising the best people.

TABLE 3: MANAGING DIVERSITY AS A SOURCE OF COMPETITIVE ADVANTAGE: THE BUSINESS ARGUMENT

Employee Issues
- Decreased turnover and absenteeism
- Easier to recruit scarce and best employees
- Decreasing workplace friction
- Improved employee relations and less stress on management
- Lower overall labour costs

Customer Issues
- Increased sales to untapped customer groups
- Employees make fewer false assumptions about customer groups and less stereotyping
- Improved understanding of customer groups and quality of service
- Enhanced public image
- Improved new product development and joint venture opportunities

Organisational Issues
- Increased innovation
- Better teamwork and lateral problem-solving
- Skills in flexibility and responsiveness

This is borne out by the statistics cited in Chapter 2, analyses of demographic changes in the workforce, the academic performance of women, the escalating workforce participation of women with children and the rising number of women who do not have children, and the success rate of women-led entrepreneurial ventures. Businesses which manage the diversity of their workforce well will not only recruit and retain the best people, they will also accrue financial and other benefits from having a harmonious workplace. The second set of incentives for managing diversity flow from the imperatives of a changing and highly differentiated market. Organisations, it is argued, should contain among their employees at least the diversity they are seeking to tap in their markets. Female car purchasers, for example, want to buy cars from manufacturers that include female designers and sales staff who understand their needs. Female banking clients want financial products designed by women who won't make inaccurate assumptions about their circumstances or abilities. The final business argument for managing diversity uses research evidence to show that diversity in organisations is correlated with greater openness and innovation. Companies that are truly diverse are less likely to become captives of narrow mindsets and the kind of 'group think' that can limit homogeneous, concurrence-seeking groups.

In both scholarship and practice the Australian 'business case for diversity' is different to that mounted in the United States, for reasons which include the legal context and racial history as well as differences in business culture. In Australia, typically, there is less emphasis put on the costs of discrimination and more on the multi-cultural nature of the workforce and the opportunities this presents to build markets and operations overseas, specifically in the geographically close Asian region.

Although these benefits are well elaborated at the level of public policy and political rhetoric, research suggests that Australian companies don't make good use of the diversity in their workforce (Office of Multicultural Affairs 1993; Hay 1996). A study by Dagher and D'Netto (1997) of 119 Australian manufacturing organisations (a sector chosen because of a high concentration of overseas-born employees) revealed an 'average' ranking in the presence, use and implementation of diversity practices. Investigating human resource practices in the areas of recruitment, training, performance appraisal and remuneration, the study found that few practices had been designed with diversity in mind. The most positive findings showed a commitment to fairness and equality in wages paid, for example, although the authors considered this to be a legacy of strong union representation rather than management commitment to diversity. The authors conclude: 'Organisations in Australia do not appear to recognise the benefits that result from effective management of workforce diversity' (1997: 11).

Practices which fit under the umbrella of diversity management often seem to be initiated as reactive problem-solving rather than strategic planning. Indeed various reports show that the emphasis of

Australian companies tends to be in the areas of helping overseas-born employees assimilate better into workplaces with language, basic skills and technical training. There are only isolated examples of companies actively drawing on the knowledge and experience of overseas-born workers to build understanding of markets or develop networks into new markets.

Limited corporate utilisation of cultural diversity in the workplace highlights the limitations of relying on simple logic to drive changes in practice. Given the homogeneity of Australian leadership and management (see Chapters 1 and 2), it becomes clear that underlying beliefs and assumptions mitigate the strength of economic logic to drive change.

Managers will, as we know, tend to trust and reward others who are like them (Eagly and Johnson 1990; Eagly 1992; Stroh *et al.* 1992). Even in decisions about promotion potential, the homosocial reproduction which Kanter identified persists (Landau 1995). Individuals feel more comfortable working in teams with others who are like them. Diverse teams experience more conflict and offer less emotional rewards for their members, even if they are more innovative in problem-solving over the medium term (Tsui, Egan and O'Reilly 1992).

If economic logic and human capital arguments prevailed, if labour markets worked as they should and no irrational restrictive practices occurred, then there would be no need for this book. However, as I concluded in Chapter 2, leadership continues to be narrowly defined, reproducing itself and resisting change. In order to more fully understand both why so little change has occurred so far and what the future holds, we need to go below the level of logic and beyond gross statistics into people's everyday experiences of difference.

Changing Practices versus Changing Attitudes

Attitudes are 'seldom changed by logic' (Henderson 1994: 137). I concluded in the opening sections of this chapter that rational and compelling arguments about resources and human capital seem to have produced little change in the way differences in workforces are managed. If we can't rely on logic or rational argument, what might stimulate attitudinal change?

Understandings about how change happens and should happen are inextricably tied to one's assumptions about the source of sex and gender differences and about how those differences are transposed, under some circumstances, into discrimination. At one extreme are those who see differences as an inevitable product of in-born biological and physiological characteristics. As the bearers and often rearers of children, women's lives and careers inevitably take different courses according to this view. The secondary-career path or 'mommy track' (Schwartz 1989), which many women experience, is a product of biological differences which cannot be changed and the best solution is for organisations to rationally accommodate and plan for these differences.

Many more theorists focus on the effects of childhood socialisation as key determinants of perceptions of difference. They see the possibility of change in processes of education and in minimising sex-role stereotyping among boys and girls.

At the opposite extreme are those who argue that gender differences that are the basis for discriminatory treatment are the result of social and structural forces which ensure that the interests of a homogenous male élite are advanced. It is not sex-based differences that are important but the way gender roles and gender stereotypes are formed and reproduced. Through the overt tools of public policy, as well as tacit social norms about, for example, women as primary caregivers, societies and organisations are structured in ways that ensure women are kept relatively powerless in families as well as organisations, and in the service of men.

At a management level, further debate surrounds the question of whether changing procedures and practices will stimulate changed attitudes, or whether more ambitious management should aim to change underlying values, norms and attitudes themselves. A large management literature and consulting industry is built on the belief that attitudinal change can be stimulated through changes in behaviour. For example, 'total quality management' and 'business process re-engineering' are based on the assumption that if behavioural processes and practices are modified then deeper attitudinal or 'cultural' change follows.

The view one takes on behaviour-led or attitudinal change depends on where one sits in disciplinary and professional terms, as well as one's cultural background and political beliefs. For example, United States practitioners of 'diversity management' generally have high expectations of managerial prerogative and the legal system to demand and then enforce behavioural compliance with non-discriminatory practices and procedures. People from European, Middle Eastern or some Asian cultures might regard such expectations as misguided, ineffective and, with some justification, likely to produce a backlash. They might argue that employees may conform to the legality of a stipulated procedure but will simultaneously undermine imposed requirements through attitudinal resistance, minimal compliance and, perhaps, subtle sabotage.

In *Trials at the Top* I borrowed the metaphor of an onion to describe organisational culture—its outer layers of practices and behaviours more amenable to change and its inner layers of attitudes, norms and values more resistant (see Hofstede *et al.* 1990). Suggesting that changes in gender attitudes are more deeply rooted and resistant to change than many other business practices and habits, I argued that the need for a combination of 'outside in' change (in practices and behaviours required by organisational leadership) and 'inside out' change (in underlying attitudes, norms and values mediated by reflection on personal experience).

My emphasis in the next section is on 'inside out' change—the changing lives of men and women which are prompting them to reassess values and expectations long taken for granted about the roles of men and women. This emphasis arises from my disciplinary background and interests, as well as my research. While I am not suggesting that these are the only forces for change, I believe they are a critical ingredient of societal change and are often overlooked in analyses which focus on structural or managerial issues.

The Experiences of Men

Men's understanding of their masculinity is woven into their lives— from family influences of fathers and grandfathers through to the daily business of working (see Andrew Tolson's pioneering study *The*

Limits of Masculinity 1977). My argument in this book has been that the sources of individual change lie in the experiences of men in their daily lives, which provoke them to unravel and reform the intricate links between their masculine identity and working and leading in a heroic way.

A study of senior managers in a housing authority points to an overwhelming reluctance among men 'to give up even partially what amounted to an addiction to the pace, power and prestige of work . . . There was no radical rethinking of the place of work in their lives' (French 1995: 63–4). Although French found some anxiety about personal health and family relationships among these managers, this was outweighed by their job satisfaction and the intense sense of belonging which their current way of working bestowed. As with my research with senior Australian executives and leaders, the majority of these managers don't see a problem with how they work, how it affects their wider lives, or how it excludes others, women and men, who can't or won't subscribe to the same norms.

Despite an espoused and apparently genuine desire to retain women in their organisation, French's managers exhibited in their own lives no understanding of juggling work and family roles and no desire to do so. The only exceptions to this general pattern were:

* a manager in a dual-career marriage whose partner was agitating for greater equality in domestic responsibilities;
* black managers who had experienced discrimination themselves;
* a male manager who was a single parent.

In one other case, a manager's views on sexual harassment had changed from impatience to understanding through his discussions with a respected woman subordinate who was the complainant. In each case it was only through direct experience or close personal involvement that these managers could 'see' the problem of systemic inequalities in the organisation and respond with a (sometimes reluctant) capacity to change their own patterns of behaviour and belief.

Australian examples of how changes in men's understandings of gender relations is mediated by personal, rarely institutional, experience are described in Chapter 4. Among the most powerful of these involve relationships with adult children, and notably daughters. This may be an artefact of the sample of CEOs we studied—most old enough to have children in their twenties, wrestling with workplaces and calling fathers to account for how the world of work is. However, other researchers, for example Steve Biddulph (1994; 1997), have built into their work on masculinities the recognition that it is in relationships with children that we not only see ourselves afresh, but are able to find the incentives to challenge and change otherwise accepted beliefs.

Fathers and Daughters*

Men reserve for, and expose to, their daughters a special side of themselves. Daughters' opinions matter and daughters' experiences touch fathers deeply. There are three, not necessarily mutually exclusive, explanations for the unique dynamics of this relationship.

One explanation is that men trust their daughters (as they rarely trust their partners and wives) to give them an especially sympathetic hearing, to value the 'real' them. Daughters have seen fathers, and accepted them, at their most vulnerable moments. They are not awed by the badges of status and they know very well what lies behind the self-importance enshrined in the executive role. Daughters are thus able to demand a special emotional accountability from their fathers. Fathers, in return, expect or just hope that their daughters will be kind. A shared history, resulting in a complicit trust, partially explains why daughters are mens' most important audience.

In the past, good relationships between fathers and daughters were those in which fathers were protective of daughters' physical and sexual safety. Daughters were dutiful, sometimes taking over the role of mother as father's carer and confidante. Although there are still traces of this, as well as the ever-present shadow of incest, women's access to greater economic and intellectual independence has expanded the basis of father–daughter relations beyond obligation and duty. Contemporary daughters can, on occasion, treat their father's views with contempt. It is precisely this fact that demands, in return, paternal respect. Perhaps this greater freedom

---

*   These ideas originally appeared as an article, 'My daughter, my self' in the *Australian Financial Review*, 24 May 1995, p. 19.

and equality also enables fathers to enjoy their daughters, with fewer fears of transgressing sexual taboos.

A second explanation of why daughters influence fathers was offered by chief executives in the *Trials at the Top* research. It concerns daughters' experiences when they venture into the world of work and encounter discrimination or harassment. In this event, it is daughters' experiences which transform, in managerial minds, what was a bothering statistic into an outrageous exclusion of half the workforce (and educational performance indicates the more intelligent half). Daughters' experiences thus enable men to see (or more significantly feel) discrimination in a direct way. A sleight on a daughter's ability is experienced as a personal affront.

Why are daughters the focus of men's emotional identification in this way, rather than sons? While daughters may inhabit the same work world as fathers, their respective achievements are less often compared as rivals. Father–daughter relationships are thus not mired by the Oedipal jockeying of fathers and sons, nor tainted by the self-sacrifice and bitterness which often underwrites relations between women and their mothers.

A third explanation centres on a process psychoanalysts call projection. In simplified terms this means that men see in their daughters a (repressed) part of themselves. Beyond what is sometimes labelled the 'feminine side', this aspect of themselves is all the more arresting in its emotional impact because it is rarely allowed expression in the world of business. Fathers project on to daughters their hankering after a less limiting and onerous path through life and work. Men see in their daughters a passion, a wilfulness, a free-spirit or a sensitivity that is unencumbered by the onerous responsibilities and layers of sobriety which can be the legacy of a lifetime in business. Daughters don't censor their views when they tell their father what they think—about women, politics or the environment. A part of many men longs for this.

I argued in *Trials at the Top* that while one of the functions the executive culture customarily served is to offer a definition of successful masculine identity, many managers are starting to question this test of executive eligibility against a heroic standard. From my research, and from other quarters, an alternative view emerges of executives as prisoners of a role and culture which forces men to conceal sides of themselves in order to survive. Some managers and leaders are growing increasingly frustrated with organisational norms and practices which exclude those who choose to express their identity and aspirations, indeed their masculinity, other than through a stoic and emotionally mute heroism.

Concerns expressed about daughters might well signal an emerging discontent with an identity increasingly anachronistic in its managerial and masculine expression.

Mothers and Sons

Relations between mothers and sons are also undergoing profound changes, which affect the models of masculinity taken up by young men. Increasingly sons are growing up with little or no contact with fathers. Mothers are also less likely to stand by and watch fathers discipline sons and inculcate masculine values in traditional ways. These changes mean that young men's notions of masculinities and apprenticeship into manhood may be mediated by women. Although Biddulph, and Bly before him, argue that this leaves young men without positive role models, these changes may well have contributed to the dynamism and experimentation in masculinities that underpins various mens movements.

Babette Smith in *Mothers and Sons* (1995) finds some evidence for shifts in the way women mother sons. The older sons in her book, in their late thirties and forties, are disturbingly distant towards and uninterested in their mothers. Commonly, these sons are dutiful, if distracted, when dealing with their mothers. Smith argues that mothers should shoulder some of the blame for perpetuating a tough and unexpressive masculinity in their sons. In extreme cases, the sons are scathing—which makes terrifying reading for mothers.

However, Smith finds much change going on, with younger sons (late teens and twenties) and younger mothers pioneering a more companionable and respectful relationship. Mothers who also work and have careers are not impeding their relationship with sons;

rather, this seems to be a basis for sons' respect. Mothers are learning how to foster different kinds of relationships with sons as they become adults, leave home, develop relationships and start families. Sons, in turn, demonstrate attitudes much freer of traditional sex-role stereotypes than those of their fathers. They enjoy cooking and are supportive of partners' careers. They want to participate in parenting and are more choosy about job options which subjugate quality of life for career.

The Experiences of Women

I have presented evidence of increasing numbers of women seeking to combine organisational leadership with a stronger assertion of their values, interests and needs as women. And I have argued that there is a trend away from the strategy of assimilation and camouflage which, for good reasons, has been the tactic of the earliest women pioneering new paths in corporations.

These positive trends, which recognise the diversity among women, have not, of course, been simply a matter of women choosing to be more assertive or courageous. That women now have a little more choice about how they pursue their careers is partially the result of structural changes. Legislation such as the Affirmative Action and Sex Discrimination Acts requires organisations to recognise systemic discrimination and take steps to remedy it, and changes in awards and leave entitlements enable women to combine parenting with career and with more equivalent rates of pay. Other societal changes, such as efforts to attract women into wider areas of undergraduate study and to make them less repellent to women, have also contributed to the broader range of career options which young women envisage for themselves and the confidence with which they plan adult lives.

The view that change is more likely once a 'critical mass' of numbers of women exist in a workplace is a commonly held view. Initially based on her pioneering work on the disabling effects of organisational tokenism, Kanter argued that some of the most powerful discriminatory effects flowed from being a lone woman in a group of men. 'Tokens' experience much greater visibility, exaggeration of their difference and increased stereotyping. These effects translate into increased performance pressures—with expectations that a token will speak for, and that her performance will stand for, all other members of her minority group. On the other hand, the presence of a token has the effect of making the dominant group much more cohesive. Their differences dissolve and are replaced by a tendency to exaggerate in-group norms and 'boundary heightening' (1977: 229), with tokens subject to extra tests of their loyalty and commitment.

Both number and proportion of women are important considerations, and Kanter argues that the stresses on tokens can reduce if there are two women in a group. Where there is a critical mass, the tendency to sex-role stereotype reduces, a broader range of behaviours is seen as acceptable and women feel a greater sense of belonging and a reduced sense of exclusion.

There is both empirical and anecdotal evidence to support the critical mass argument. For example, in a study of senior women in eight United States law firms, Ely (1995) found that in more male-dominated firms senior women evaluated feminine attributes more negatively, rated men as more masculine and experienced more strongly sexualised gender roles. In 'sex-integrated' law firms (with a higher proportion of female partners), women regarded feminine attributes more favourably and were able to draw on both masculine and feminine aspects of themselves to deal with different problems. Ely also found that 'women in sex-integrated firms believed that expressing their individuality would contribute to their success, whereas those in male-dominated firms believed such behavior would be a hindrance' (1995: 626).

Ely's work underlines that sex roles are not static and are not a property which the individual controls and projects. Rather, what is judged as appropriate and effective behaviour by women is constructed within each workplace setting and constantly being negotiated.

In my work with executives and managers, I have had an opportunity to observe the contrasts between groups of public-sector managers (in which women are from 30 to 50 per cent of participants) and other programmes in which there are sometimes as few as one or two women in a group of fifty or sixty male participants. The content of the sessions is general management and organisational issues, rather than gender. However, two things are worth noting. In the groups where there are only one or two women, gender is a taboo topic. The women's strategy is typically one of camouflage and commonly they say little. If they do speak, even about the same amount as male participants, they are perceived as 'standing out'. Where women make up about a third of a group, however, relations between men and women, or gender aspects of leadership style, will often be raised by participants for discussion.

Further, and as Kanter predicted, there is evidently space in these groups for women to be more individual—for some to be vocal and talk a lot and for others to be more thoughtful and measured in their contributions; for some to dress in a distinctive way and for others to be very extroverted; for some to be more strongly feminine in their attributes and others masculine, and so on.

Evidence thus supports aspects of the critical mass argument. Women are less constrained and trapped within stereotypes and assumptions about how women 'should be' when there are more of them. While women benefit from having more women around them, there is still little evidence that this will produce pervasive cultural change. Neither should the evidence be taken to mean that 'number balancing' is an efficacious way of ending sex discrimination (Ely 1995: 589). Discrimination is a very complex compound of direct and indirect effects, only one set of which is addressed by having a critical mass or greater representation of women.

While acknowledging Kanter's arguments, a number of researchers advocate a broader understanding of systemic power in workplaces. An analysis of the organisational order of male dominance needs to explain how women came to have so little power and men so much. A structural analysis, according to Cynthia Cockburn, should explore the way 'the societal gender order and society-wide systems of racial domination penetrate the workplace where individuals act as vectors of power across the boundaries between the organization and the outside world' (1990: 86).

Cockburn is one of a number in *Men, Masculinities and Social Theory* who vest their hopes for change in a more radically based shift of consciousness among men. Cockburn concludes:

If gender and race oppression have their being as much outside as inside the organization, and if individual agency is effective on or in organizations, surely we cannot avoid in the long run the problem of changing consciousness, which essentially means winning defectors from power systems (1990: 88).

Any analysis of change thus needs to take a wide perspective. It needs to applaud, and pay attention to, the small changes in the way individual men and women combine work and families; and changes in the way individual managers draw on their personal experiences to build better workplaces for women and other minority groups. Understanding the dynamics of individual change are critical to overcoming resistances and developing programmes for change which have good chances of success.

At the same time, structural variables are central. To portray change as simply a matter of individual determination is to wildly overstate people's choices and underestimate systemic obstacles and distribution of power within organisations. I have been at conferences where the general tone of advice to aspiring women is 'Just go for it!' While not wanting to dampen optimism, this seems the ludicrously simplified exhortation of the privileged and (relatively) powerful.

The broader economic and political environment creates the context for the possibility of change. At the end of the twentieth century Australia, like many industrialised countries, is experiencing pressures to reduce the costs of regulation to business, and organisations are dramatically reducing numbers of employees—resulting in improved productivity but an erosion of traditional employee benefits. These shifts in economic, regulatory and business ideology are likely to have profound effects on the progress of women as regulatory safety-nets are removed and individual women are given the onus to demonstrate, in supposedly objective tests of performance, their economic value.

A likely response to these economic and business changes will be an accelaration of the already-marked movement of women out of large corporations and into medium-sized and small operations, often set up and managed by women institutionalising a different way of working.

Ultimately, structural and cultural change, behavioural and attitudinal change, 'outside in' and 'inside out' change, systemic change and changes in the lives and working environments of individual women and men, need to work in tandem to work at all. As Tolson summarises his exploration of masculinity in Britain: 'the experience of individual men is constituted by a whole system of work and domestic life. And the transformation of this system, including its "gender-roles", must remain a collective responsibility' (1977: 144).

. . .

This chapter has explored some deeper explanations of why change in gender relations in organisations and the structure of leadership has encountered resistance and, some would say, been so achingly slow.

Many people in positions of power to lead change don't experience discrimination and consequently don't see the need for change. Underlying this basis of resistance are probably more deep-seated desires to keep organisations defined as masculine domains through rejection of what is perceived as feminine. This preserves a deep sense of gender order, keeping power in the hands of those accustomed to having it and ensuring that many men benefit from a minimal share of domestic labour and family responsibilities. Some women also reject change because they perceive that they gain more from subscribing to the status quo.

For change to happen, two sets of forces need to coalesce. Structural changes—in the power and positions taken up by women, and in the legislative structure which supports struggles for equality of pay and access to family leave—are among those necessary. Mostly, these structural initiatives work by identifying and sanctioning discriminatory processes and rewarding changes in organisational practices.

However, I have argued that changes in the attitudes of men are critical underpinnings to broader change. These are predominantly 'inside out' changes through which men are provoked, encouraged or forced to rethink the links between their masculine identity and their way of working—their values and priorities. This rethinking takes many routes: through coming to terms with sexualities; through negotiating the tensions of a dual-career marriage or partnership;

through the experiences or outlooks of a daughter or son; through illness and a re-ordering of life's priorities; through loss of a job or career; through divorce or loss of a partner; through a close friend's or colleague's battle against discrimination. Having children in a first, or second, relationship can also provoke a sense of wanting to father better—and perhaps better than men were fathered themselves.

Examples of Australian male leaders navigating this new territory of combining leadership with a different sort of life were discussed in Chapter 4. This analysis shows that while the nexus between masculine and work identity remains unexamined, it is unlikely that the majority of men's attitudes will change. While the régime of most organisations and the social division of family labour continue to support men defining themselves through an extraordinarily high commitment to career, then change is unlikely.

Structural and individual changes must reinforce one another. We are seeing gradual structural changes, as society and organisations roll back obstacles to both men and women experimenting with different strategies. They include the extension and take-up of paternity leave, and actions against organisations that penalise parents, in various subtle ways, for taking family leave. Much rests on whether organisational leaders, given a mandate for change, will see the centrality of gender relations to unlocking archaic work cultures.

9 TOWARDS A THEORY OF LEADERSHIP AND SEXUALITY

For many male leaders, leadership has also been an accomplishment of masculinity, with a traditional but invisible link between enactment of a particular heterosexual masculinity, self-esteem and leadership. For women, leadership has mostly required the active censorship or camouflage of female sexuality.

Drawing on my research, I argue that this habitual response of camouflage is changing. A model is proposed in this chapter which identifies a relationship between power and sexuality in leadership, showing how as women acquire power in organisations they have greater choice in the extent to which they either deny and camouflage their womanliness or express their difference in the way they lead. There are, I conclude, an increasing range of ways senior women are bringing their womanliness—their sexual identities and sexualities —to leadership.*

Defining Sexuality

Leadership has, despite consuming research scrutiny, escaped from being sexualised. For example, Bass and Stogdill's *Handbook of Leadership* (1990), which runs to over a thousand pages and accommodates modest entries on gender, masculinity and sex-role stereotypes in leadership research, fails to mention sexuality. This is not comforting reassurance that sexuality isn't important in leadership —rather that the concept of leadership is sexuality-blind.

Social theorists and feminists have revisited and reconstituted psychoanalytic understandings of sexuality (for example, de Beauvoir 1953; Lacan 1966; Mitchell 1975; Foucault 1981; Irigaray 1993; Chodorow 1994). Juliet Mitchell, introducing Lacan's work, argues

---

* This chapter is adapted from my article in *International Review of Women and Leadership* 1(2), 1995.

that sexuality should never be equated with biology or genitality, but rather is 'always about psychosexuality' (1982: 2). Sexuality is an expression, conscious and unconscious, of who one is, with particular emphasis on physicality, gender identity, aspiration and fantasy. Expressing one's sexuality is a source of satisfaction which can arise in many ways and from various sources—some of which are legitimised, while others are not.

In the context of organisations, sexuality has often been misdefined as sexual affairs or sexual harassment. The result has been, as Burrell (1984) has observed, that organisations set out to suppress sexuality, propelled by the misguided management fantasy that sex 'like scurvy' can be eradicated from workplaces (Burrell and Hearn 1989). But sex and work are not easy to separate. As Lobel (1993) has noted, characteristics of effective relationships, such as trust and openness, are the same ingredients which promote sexual attraction and involvement. Research indicates that a large number of people meet their sexual partners through work. The impossibility of eradicating sex from organisations highlights the need to shift focus to understanding more deeply how sexualities manifest themselves in organisations, and how some are accepted and even permeate organisational cultures while others are deeply threatening and rigidly proscribed.

The definition of sexuality I propose seeks to recognise a much wider array of sexualities expressed in organisations and in leadership: sexuality as good and bad; as willed and as imposed; as imprisoning and potentially liberating. It enables us to bring to the surface the link between an assumed sexuality and hegemony in leadership theory and practice, and to reveal the suppression of other sexualities.

Masculine Heterosexualities and Leadership

Men's sexual behaviour in organisations exists yet is taken for granted, labelled and understood as normal boisterousness (Gutek 1982; 1985). Organisational sexual behaviours by men are described as 'boys being boys', 'letting off steam' or 'being part of the team'— and are therefore constructed as conducive to organisational performance. These behaviours then become entrenched in cultural rituals, symbols and practices (Sheppard 1989; Collinson 1992). They become part of doing the work.

In her study of secretaries and their bosses, Rosemary Pringle (1988) has also importantly shown how male heterosexuality has been made invisible in organisational life:

> Men are seen as rational, analytic, assertive and competitive, but not as sexual beings. Women, on the other hand, are seen in almost exclusively sexual terms and it is they who are assumed to 'use' their sexuality at work (Pringle 1992: 99).

Subsequent researchers have begun to unearth the often quite extensive but, to management, invisible expression of sexualities woven into organisational cultures. In the study of strategic management in financial services discussed in Chapter 4, Kerfoot and Knights conclude sexuality to be 'an ordinary and frequently public process rather than an extraordinary feature of private life' (1993: 669). Indeed, they document the way corporate initiatives, such as team-building, channel expressions of intimacy and closeness towards the expression of corporate goals. Rather than the suppression of sexualities, 'strategic management could be said to utilize sexuality in its operation' (1993: 670). From his studies of senior managers, Roper argues the need to look much deeper at how men express their sexuality and intimacy at work, taking issue with a widely accepted portrayal of managers as rational and impersonal, therefore stoic and unfeeling. He concludes that, to a far greater extent than acknowledged, 'homo-erotically charged feelings' influence all sorts of management decisions, from succession planning to acquisition approvals (1996: 213).

In another example, Barrett (1996) shows how a hierarchy of masculinities and sexualities reinforces lines of authority in the navy. The élite group in the navy (in cultural if not bureaucratic terms) are the 'fly boys' or pilots. Their élitism is sustained via the most aggressive macho-heterosexuality. The mystique of flying highly dangerous missions involves mastery of multi-million dollar machinery, and feelings which teeter between the sacred and the erotic. Their experiences are treated with reverence beyond expression. The potency of these naval leaders is sustained through sexualised imagery, and a hierarchy of sexualities in which this group stands at the top.

Share trading and dealing sections of the financial services industry provide particularly graphic examples of the interweaving of sexualities and leadership. Highly pressured environments and long hours, it is argued, have the effect of reducing inhibitions. The legacy is that the high-flyers and 'gun traders' often mark their prowess through sexualised rituals and language. Sexual degradation of female and junior male traders is often part of reproducing the hierarchy.

Leadership is not an asexual activity. Chapters 3 and 4 demonstrate that the enactment of leadership in many organisations resonates with and is sustained by particular expressions of male sexualities. These expressions derive from organisational cultures, giving emphasis to differing values of competitivism, intimacy and bonding, heterosexual conquest or, more implicitly, keeping women in their place. Just as Collinson and Hearn conclude that 'organizations provide significant social contexts and resources through which instances of men's sexualities can be enacted' (1994: 7), I want to suggest that the practice of leadership has also provided continuing and varied opportunities for the expression of male sexualities. Effective leadership is not devoid of sexuality but is partially established by subtle yet powerful expressions of sexualities.

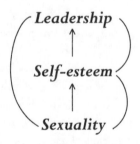

FIGURE 1: THE RELATIONSHIP BETWEEN SEXUALITY AND LEADERSHIP FOR MOST MEN.

Nor is it coincidental that charismatic leaders rely on aspects of their sexual attractiveness (to both men and women), such as their stature, voice, bearing and charm. The power and influence of organisational leaders cannot be considered without recognition of the sexual dimensions to their leadership.

Leadership, Sexuality and Self-esteem

Leadership theory has been built on a bedrock of association between constructs of achievement and masculinity. Masculinity was measured and operationalised in psychological tests, such as the Bem Sex Role Inventory, in opposition to femininity. Further, psychological research indicates a strong correlation between individuals' self-esteem, masculinity and achievement on the one hand (Bem 1974; 1981), and between self-esteem and leadership on the other. For men, sexual identity and self-esteem have the potential to be correlated and mutually reinforcing in leadership (see Figure 1).

Women's Sexuality in Leadership

Femininity remains a perjorative term among most managers (male and female) because it conveys the opposite of leadership. If there is one thing that has often united feminists and liberal female managers it is the desire to avoid the label 'feminine', because it simultaneously defines one as ineffective. At the same time, women's reluctance to be labelled 'feminist' (Weiner 1995) has also been widely noted, because of its connotations within patriarchal discourse. The conversion of femaleness, within the dominant discourse, into radical extremism (feminism) or frivolous ineffectiveness (femininity) leaves women with few ways of describing their womanliness that are not liabilities from a leadership perspective.

In *The Second Sex* (1953), Simone de Beauvoir showed that masculinity and femininity are not equally balanced opposites. In leadership too, masculinity is valorised and reinforced. Femininity, on the other hand, is so out of place when we think of management that it borders on the absurd. 'The concept man manager makes little sense . . . A woman must disassociate herself from those features which define her femininity in other spheres . . . [women] have to reproduce a management self which is symbolized by the opposite of what they are supposed to be' (Swan 1994: 106–7).

A strong sense of sexual identity can be a liability for women in leadership roles. Attractiveness tends to increase the likelihood of a woman being sex-role stereotyped as frivolous, as a token or as a sex object (Schein 1973 and 1975; Kanter 1977). Gutek and Morasch (1982) explain how sex and sexuality for women who are a minority in job roles can prompt sexual harassment. They use the concept of sex-role spillover to show that when there are one or two women among many men (as is commonly the case in management roles), the sex of the women, rather than other attributes, becomes salient.

In contrast to many men, who experience a reinforcing relationship between sexuality, self-esteem and leadership, women may have to work to establish leadership by uncoupling their sexual identity from their leadership persona or minimising the salience of their sex. Traditionally, women have accomplished this by, for example, dressing innocuously or cultivating an androgynous demeanour, by rarely referring to or allowing themselves to be typecast as representing 'women's issues' or 'being one of the boys', by repressing emotion or by selectively absenting themselves from executive rituals (see Sheppard 1989 for further examples). Through this process the female leader may be systematically deprived of sources of

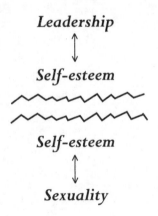

FIGURE 2: THE RELATIONSHIP BETWEEN SEXUALITY AND LEADERSHIP FOR WOMEN

self-esteem and confidence which would naturally tend to accrue to men in her position (see Figure 2).

Sexuality and Power Among Women

Figure 3 sets out the ways women respond to the complex pressures of leadership and sexuality described above. The model consists of two dimensions:

- the extent to which sexuality and sexual persona is recognised as an important part of the work self;
- the extent to which women have some power in how that sexuality is expressed.

The significance of power in shaping sexual options was elaborated by Kanter in *Men and Women of the Corporation* (1977). How women express their sexual selves is negotiated within a cultural and political system determined by their power (for example, whether they are chief executives), their characteristics and how they are seen within the organisation (older women's sexuality is generally seen as more benign). In contrast to Kanter, however, I want to suggest that the positions adopted by women are a matter of both power and sexual awareness.

Around the two core dimensions in Figure 3 are four quadrants. To move through the four quadrants would be to tread a path of developing consciousness accompanied by increasing power. In accounts of their careers, women often start out expecting that sexuality will not be an issue at work (quadrant 1). They then become more aware of sexual meanings at work while operating within the constraints of male-defined rules of sexuality (quadrant 2). Increasing power is often accompanied by the belief that sexuality can be left behind (quadrant 3); finally, with power, some women exhibit greater forthrightness in the expression of their sexuality at work (quadrant 4). Sexuality may be expressed in dress, in speaking about different things and in a different way, in allowing personal lives and family greater expression at work. In this fourth quadrant, women are using power and sexual awareness to write the scripts of how they'll be as leaders. The four relationships of power and sexuality are described below, drawing on my research and that of others.

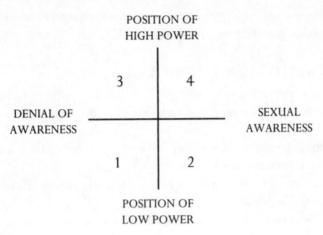

POSITION OF
HIGH POWER

3   4

DENIAL OF   SEXUAL
AWARENESS   AWARENESS

1   2

POSITION OF
LOW POWER

FIGURE 3: A MODEL OF SEXUALITY AND POWER FOR WOMEN

1. Denial of Sexuality / Low Power

In the first two quadrants women have little power. Because my interviewees were all senior women, I will rely on their recollections and on other research to describe the approaches adopted in these two quadrants.

The denial of sexuality and femaleness has been well-documented in this book and elsewhere as a very common response to working in a male culture. It is accomplished through dressing to disguise, as well as never mentioning one's private life to the point of hiding the fact of having children. Women often avoid other women, whether in administrative or professional roles, to attempt to 'pass' in predominantly male environments.

One woman, not part of this research, described her life as a bond salesman being 'one of the most humiliating jobs'. She found that the only strategy she could adopt in such a competitive and brutal environment was to 'play down your sexuality and dowdify yourself. I wore expensive suits in black, navy and grey, which I have now buried' she says (*New Woman*, July 1995).

Gordon's (1991) research of American executives is replete with examples of women learning and, more frighteningly, being trained to subjugate any trace of womanliness. Women are counselled to avoid having photographs of children on desks or taking parental leave, for fear that they will be perceived as less than fully committed to their job.

Working in circumstances of little power, some women will also deny the significance of their sex to themselves, claiming to be 'just one of the team'. As I have noted earlier, this approach is more viable when women are relatively junior in their career and the prospect of maternity has not been raised.

2. Low Power / High Sexual Awareness

Some workplace cultures are highly sexualised and they become more so when women are employed. My interviews include examples of women's sexuality being illuminated and constructed in ways designed to humiliate them or compromise their professional effectiveness. In such cases the ambient culture and women's comparative lack of power control the sexual meanings extracted from the exchange. But women in these workplaces adopt, or are compelled to take, a stance of greater sexual awareness.

According to one woman, there is acceptance of a certain sort of sexuality in the workplace:

> There have always been affairs between bosses and their secretaries, and that has been okay, because it is in the interests of the person with power . . . sex always comes back to power, well certainly in the workplace.

Others describe, particularly early in their career, encountering a prevalent ethos of affairs between powerful men and subordinate women.

Women's lack of significant power can also earn them special status as confidante:

> They often haven't got anyone to talk to—it is so closed . . . you know you might be equal in power, but you are not really, because you are a woman . . . so therefore you are not a threat . . . you are privileged to see the insights of peoples' lives in a way that not many people do.

Awareness of sexuality is expressed in a special sense of closeness with senior male colleagues. Although rarely accompanied by physical relationships, women describe times of intimacy when they felt 'privileged' and 'moved' to see sides of powerful men which few others see, either men or women. Extreme vulnerability is witnessed.

Women describe their own various responses to this magnetic intimacy—from getting 'too entangled' to trying to 'keep a little distance'. The risks are high and the experience of conforming to a sexualised role over which one has little control is ultimately an unsatisfying one for women. Although they have a sense of themselves sexually, the scripts available are limited and their power is fragile. One interviewee admitted growing very bored with the role of coaching men to be 'a good lover, a good leader, a good this and a good that', and another tired of the burden of defining and setting the limits of the relationship.

3. Denial of Sexuality / High Power

Some women acquire power, and continue to mute and submerge their sexuality. The research shows that this has typically been accomplished either by protesting that femaleness is irrelevant to success, or by conforming to a sex-role stereotype rather than being assertive of one's own sexual identity.

Examples come from interviewees talking about other women. One describes her devastation when joining a large organisation and approaching the only other senior woman:

> I went to see her and walked out of the room in shell shock. I asked her what she thought of equal opportunity—she said it was a load of crap basically . . . she said that she had been successful 'because I am a very intelligent capable woman. I have had no privilege because I was a woman'. The worst thing I could have done was go and speak to her, because then she lined me up [as an opponent and to be got rid of] . . . she has had to give away her female qualities to be successful. Then she looks at me and sees me—what she has had to give up to be where she is—of course she wouldn't want me around.

These women adopt a less threatening persona to male peers, despite their power. The stereotypes encountered in my research include the principled 'schoolmarm' (who shades into mother); the thoroughly business-like specialist (whose advice is quarantined to specific disciplinary fields or expertise); the dutiful daughter prepared to learn from older men; the tomboy 'kid sister' who plays along on the fringe of the 'boys games'.

An interviewee conveyed her observations and reservations of other women moving around this troublesome territory:

> . . . you are a little bit unsure about how to handle relationships . . . if you look at, if you like, other women as role models, you see a range of behaviours. So I am very uncomfortable with, or perhaps disapprove of the sort of, you know the kind of dumb blonde kind of stuff. People clearly trying to use feminine wiles . . . sort of burst into tears to sort of cover up, clearly where they haven't done enough work or you know, up to the mark—that makes me feel very uncomfortable . . . But equally some sort of professional women are quite flirtatious and seem to get away with that. Some do it very warm . . . warm to the point almost if you like being flirtatious, but they get away with it . . . I probably err on the more conservative side . . . in order not to be offensive, I suppose, so perhaps as I get more comfortable in myself I'll . . . it is a matter of relaxing a bit more.

The women I interviewed recognised the pull of stereotypes and the difficulty of expressing one's sexuality and womanliness in a way that repudiated the most oppressive of stereotypes. For some, the way forward lay in self-consciously assuming roles for particular purposes, in making use of the types of influence that stereotypical roles afford (see also Porter 1994). For other women it lay in selective resistance: occasional assertions and interposition of aspects of themselves to mitigate the impact of the sex-role stereotype hoisted upon them. The risk of this approach, as one of Gordon's executives described, was that she 'eventually became the character she had invented in order to succeed . . . after a while you become what you're behaving' (1991: 209).

Another of my interviewees suggested that working according to male rules, even though it involved repression of femaleness, eventually ended up feeling like 'prostitution'. This dilemma was part of the reason for increasing numbers of women leaving senior positions:

> not only because they don't think they are getting the big jobs and the rewards they deserve, but also because they think there is too much bullshit and they are not prepared to prostitute themselves to the extent that they become part of it—that they collude with that game.

A number of women found that enacting a stereotyped sexuality offered short-term influence but ultimately perpetuated powerlessness.

4. High Power / High Sexual Awareness

Yet other women combine being powerful with constituting their own meanings of sexuality as part of asserting themselves as women. In Table 4, I list some of the associations women offered when I asked about leadership and sexuality. Consistent with Juliet Mitchell's view, women offer meanings of sexuality which are tied to who they are—remote from the act of sex, or the biology of sexual difference. Overall, women felt that sexuality was something positive, an aspect of themselves that on balance was important to their identity and their life.

This had not always been the case—sexuality had often been more of a 'problem' when they were more junior or worked in an environment where their sex was constantly highlighted. However, with power had come greater choice and control about how sexuality was projected and perceived.

These women offered a wide range of responses—from anecdotes about children to incidents of sexual attraction; accounts of harassment and affairs; images of circumstances in which they felt good about themselves; circumstances in which they had observed, or overstepped, a sexual boundary at work, and feelings about the work and the excitment of working with others. Some offered a warm picture of their organisation. One admitted, 'I get really turned on by some of this stuff', feeling that 'deep down in the bosom of the company' employees, including herself, felt 'very passionate' about what they were doing.

TABLE 4: STRATEGIES FOR ALIGNING POWER WITH SEXUALITY

Specialness: the sense of being a woman among men
- having privileged access to men
- being a confidante and advisor to powerful men

Being attracted to people at work
- spillover from intense work collaboration
- closeness, travelling with work colleagues, intimacy
- flirtation
- sexual relationships

Being at the hub of a work group, being confident and in control
- satisfaction in seeing others blossom
- being needed and sought after
- shaping the business, the excitment of leading and making things happen

Physicality and strength
- looking good
- exercising: swimming, running, walking, aerobics etc.
- being outdoors, in touch with the environment
- being physically strong and capable

Being with other women
- networks with women outside the organisation
- links as mentor, mentee, sponsor, role model, friend to women in the organisation
- friends with whom to talk about work and other things
- female family and extended family members: mothers, sisters etc.
- women as partners and sexual partners

TABLE 4 *contd*

Individuality in dress
- using dress to express individuality: 'a bit hippy', use of colour, wearing pants
- not subjugating self to corporate anonymity

Family
- talking to partners, being affectionate and intimate
- attachment to children and, if adult, their children
- being pregnant and bringing babies to work
- having older children come to work

Artistic pursuits and interests
- playing a musical instrument, painting etc.

Spirituality
- looking after oneself, achieving balance
- meditation

For another woman, a new path emerged from a rejection of traditional stereotypes and a 'phony' view of femininity:

> . . . femininity as having a soft voice and being nice to everyone. I don't see femininity like that at all. I wrote a poem about feminin-ity. I was away at a conference and there was a group of women there who were drawing circles . . . and I wrote a poem saying femininity was barbed wire . . . [there is] this sort of *phony* view of femininity: 'we're all soft and gentle and generous and lovely. I think femininity is quite harsh and real and lively and painful.

In other cases, sexuality was expressed as sexual energy or a sense of 'being together', being yourself and whole:

> I see sexual identity as sort of sexual energy for me . . . when I have a wonderful night's sleep, done some exercise and I've eaten reasonably healthily . . . it raises my self-esteem. Then my libido starts to get itself together a bit more. Then I feel like I interact with people with great humour and warmth and you know, sometimes

flirting, but sort of with a good energy that can have a sexual over-tone and I'll wear nice things that make me feel good, but never provocative.

Expressing oneself sexually can involve outbursts of assertion, anger, even physical aggressiveness. In her study of anger among women principals, Court (1995) describes women learning how to vent anger. My interviewees told of being locked into bitter struggles with colleagues and of finding strength in their stature, their voice, their groundedness. There is not just mental toughness here but a sense of physicality which asserts itself.

Women are attuned to misusing their power in a sexual sense, particularly when a junior colleague or subordinate is involved. Powerful women tend to be cautious in situations of attraction. As one interviewee noted, 'you just cannot be so close with somebody without some kind of attraction developing'; 'fleeting fantasies' are not uncommon. The desire for, or more rarely the reality of, sexual relationships with work colleagues is a significant dimension of sexuality for some women.

One woman reflects, with the tinge of regret echoed by a number, on her 'ethic' not to become involved:

I have thought a lot about it because as most women I have got myself into really deep relationships at work and it is hard to handle that . . . we enjoyed each other's company, never touched each other, all the traditional things you do to avoid an intimate sexual encounter with somebody—you know its dangerous.

The difficulty of negotiating this territory, where sexual attraction exists but is not acted upon, also figures in other research. Lobel (1993) reports that many men and women in organisations develop very close, but not sexually intimate, relationships with colleagues. Consistent with my argument about the relationship between self-esteem, sexuality and leadership, such relationships were, in the case of men, associated with supportive effects and did not result in negative work outcomes. Women involved in such relationships were more likely to report tensions and difficulties.

As in other areas, it would seem that while there is some acceptance in organisations for men developing very close relationships with colleagues, the stakes and risks for women, especially senior women, are higher. One woman talks about the 'rules' which she formulated in discussion with a female friend, also a chief executive:

> There are a couple of things I have as *rules* and one has to be very watchful about any sort of overt, any sort of sexual connotation at work . . . People who work for me have much less power than me, you know . . . [another woman CEO] told me this . . . she said that first of all she thinks its unforgivable to tantrum and shout and yell at staff. What can they do? I mean they can't do much because you're the boss and I think that she is absolutely right . . . and the second thing is you can't be sexually provocative . . . because they can't do much. They can't say 'Look you were a bit revolting or that offended me.'

Sexuality flowed into, or was expressed through, a sense of sexual attractiveness and sexual attraction. A shared victory or special understanding inevitably creates familiarity and intimacy. Occasionally power and influence at work prompted a reappraisal of sexual identity and sexual preference. In other cases, women's experience of power and leadership reflected back into relationships with husbands and partners, acting as a prompt to redefine these relationships (for examples, see Marshall 1995).

. . .

> Man is a human being with sexuality; woman is a complete individual, equal to the male, only if she too is a human being with sexuality. To renounce her femininity is to renounce a part of her humanity. (Simone de Beauvoir 1953/1972: 691–2)

Leadership cannot be dissociated from particular expressions of sexuality. For many men in the Australian context, the enactment of leadership has been accompanied by validation of a heroic masculine heterosexuality. Simultaneously, leadership has been reinforced through the expression of particular sexualities that are so well-integrated into the culture that their sexual content goes unnoticed.

Psychological research suggests that, for some men, strong sexual identity is associated with high self-esteem and confidence, in turn related to leadership. If leading is, at least partially, a sexual activity, this finding is unproblematic for those men who enjoy the self-esteem accruing from a coincidence of a sexual identity and leadership behaviours. It is not so straightforward for those homosexual and other men who are less comfortable with displays of assertive heterosexuality.

Revealing the connection between masculine heterosexuality and leadership makes visible the ways women's sexual identities are excluded from, or censored by, constructs of leadership. Women often work in environments in which traditional leadership is supported by, and reinforces, a masculine heterosexual identity. Against this powerful yet undiscussed ingredient of leadership, women's sexualities have been experienced and cast as a problem—the cause of discrimination and harassment, requiring resources and legislation to control.

For many women, leading has required active management of the salience of their sexuality through camouflage of their sex or conformity to a stereotyped sex role. Such strategies, however, deprive women of a source of self-esteem, the expression of a confident sexual identity.

In her work, Judi Marshall observed that 'Many women now consciously want to take who they are as women into organizations' (1984: 232). She called this path one of 'creative individuality' to distinguish it from two more traditional paths of conformity and rebellion. The women I interviewed similarly endorsed the importance, to them, of a kind of powerful womanliness, a strong sense of self anchored to physicality and identity, for which I have proposed the concept of sexuality.

Women are bringing new dimensions of themselves, including expressions of sexualities, to their work. In order to capture these meanings I have proposed a model which asserts that both women's power and their forthrightness about their sexuality determines how they respond to the complex pressures encountered in leadership roles. For most of the women in my small sample, sexuality is an important aspect of who they are (though they may not label it as such). Leadership which was contingent on conformity to sex-role stereotyping was widely regarded as unsatisfactory. When they talked about their own sexuality and those of other women with whom they worked, they were clear that a sense of one's sexuality was associated with being effective and feeling good.

10
DOING IT DIFFERENTLY

Gender and sexuality have always been central and assumed components of effective leadership, yet both have been neglected in traditional leadership scholarship. In this book I have sought to illuminate these relationships, showing why they have developed and what the implications have been for the leaders of organisations and the led.

The Australian workforce is increasingly heterogeneous in gender, cultural background and ethnicity, first language and family structure. Organisational leadership, however, remains notably homogeneous in these terms. Overwhelmingly, our leaders are male, speak English as a first language and live in a nuclear family with the support of a wife. Taking gender and sexuality as its focus, this book offers explanation of how leadership homogeneity has persisted and flourished, despite the most rational economic arguments, and of how it might change.

Critical to my argument is the need to deconstruct the traditional but obscured relationship between heroic masculinity and corporate leadership. Until we unravel and expose the links between being a leader and enacting a particular form of manliness, then, in gender and racial terms, leadership will remain the domain of a homogenous élite.

In a field with such a vast literature and pool of scholars, it is daunting, perhaps naive, to argue for a new concept of leadership. However, work in the areas of gender and sexualities has the capacity to give us new and radical ways of understanding patterns we have come to take for granted. It is precisely constructs like leadership, about which we assume so much has been done that nothing new can be said, where a gender perspective can offer rich and deep insights.

Constructed Leadership

Leadership can be best understood as a phenomenon constructed in the minds and eyes of the audience, as much as in the deeds and character of the observed leader. The process of construction begins early in life, with our infantile pitting of overwhelming dependence against the power of the primary carer, usually the mother. Right from the start, gender has been on the agenda of leadership.

I have used the term 'archetype of leadership' to capture the collective, constructed and unconscious dimensions of leadership. Fathers and Mothers are the first archetypes of male and female leaders. They provide powerful and enduring templates of where we see leadership and how we feel about it.

My research, joining other work, highlights the legacy that the first encounter with female leadership often leaves. Mothers may be admired for their strength, but we forgive them for less than the first male leaders in our lives. Fathers thus enjoy an affection derived from greater distance and independence, as well as lower expectations. When mothers are interested in us, we don't notice because it is what we expect. When they ignore us or let us down, there is a sense of profound betrayal. Fathers burden us less with their expectations and demands, and when they are attentive it is more likely that we will be able to receive their interest with gratitude and grace.

Partially because of these early, and inevitable, exchanges, female leaders are typically regarded with more ambivalence than male leaders. For many audiences, women in authority or leadership roles resonate with early frustrations and unmet demands; they reactivate the conflict between our need to be nurtured and our drive to be independent. Powerful women, I have argued, are magnets for the largely unconscious ambivalences about mothers and the feminine that both men and women feel.

I also argue that the centrality of gender and sexuality of leadership has been systematically obscured. Luce Irigaray, the French philosopher, says that sexual difference is the major philosophical issue of our age (1993). Postmodern perspectives inform my argument here, with their insistence on the existence of constructed and multiple truths. The focus of postmodernism on language and power helps to reveal how the rhetoric of leadership becomes self-perpetuating, leaving little room for a different truth about leadership to be revealed.

Men, Women and Leadership

Research on gender identities has revealed how one construct of masculinity becomes dominant—and de-legitimises and marginalises alternative masculinities. In Chapters 3 and 4, I chart the evolution of a particular understanding of masculinity in the definition of executive leadership. Our attachment to a heroic ideal of leadership is deeply rooted in Australian cultural mythology. Historical accounts and popular folklore have elevated our belief in the redemptive powers of solitary, courageous men who triumph through endurance, stamina and self-reliance.

The same qualities are still widely celebrated, as they should be, in many aspects of Australian life. Yet in the subtle but powerful processes of selecting and reproducing executive leadership, the necessary qualifications for leadership have become increasingly narrow. Executive leadership has come to be identified with a tough stoicism, a rejection of the sentimental and the feminine, a belief that the heroism of the bottom line and the balance sheet is revealed through a phlegmatic and solitary leadership. There is talk of teams, but these are competitive devices for the extraction of fierce accountability, emptied of genuine collaboration (Sinclair 1995e). There are also 'visions' but these are passionless, sterile exhortations which fail to inspire a diverse workforce or make a mark on the competitive and culturally complex global stage.

It was research of men in leadership roles that initially revealed a potentially reinforcing relationship between leadership, masculinity and sexuality. Being leaders, for many men, also accomplished a strong masculine sexual identity. Having a strong sense of being a big man among other men reinforced their identification as leaders. In both historic and contemporary corporate life, the two identities as leader and man have fitted hand-in-glove.

The equation of executive leadership with a narrow expression of masculinity is under some challenge—although not, it must be said, at the most senior levels of large organisations. Few such challenges penetrate this insulated and hallowed corporate environment.

To find examples, we must look at the pressures in personal lives, which are themselves a product of broader changes—from the economic fall-out of restructurings and downsizing to the impacts of feminism and the transformation of women's economic expectations. It is children, particularly daughters, and to a lesser degree partners and friends, who are demanding that executives think again about the way they have always been and, in turn, how they have worked and led.

For the few women in leadership roles, there has been no discernible reinforcing relationship between being a leader and being a woman. Indeed, being 'seen' as a woman diminishes one's leadership. Behaviours which draw attention to sex—such as displays of overt femininity, being pregnant, references to family, wearing colourful or expressive clothes, lobbying for women or adopting explicit feminist stances—typically diminish a woman's leadership potential in the eyes of observers. This dilemma gives aspiring female leaders an extra handicap and strips them of the potentially reinforcing source of identity and esteem which many male leaders continue to enjoy.

This explains why women, consciously and unconsciously, have used all sorts of strategies to conceal gender and sexuality, to camouflage, to blend in rather than stand out. By dressing in particular ways, by playing along with the jokes, by not supporting other women, by not allowing oneself to be associated with 'women's issues' or by seeking to minimise one's absences from the workplace for maternal or family reasons, women have sought to reduce the visibility and the impact of their gender and their sexuality.

But this strategy is self-defeating, as shown in this and other research. Women's efforts to conceal sex expose them to charges of 'trying too hard to be one of the boys'. And the constant effort of concealment deprives women of an important part of identity, a sense of self which rightly should be a central and reinforcing component of their leadership. Nor has the camouflage strategy produced other sought-after outcomes. It has not enabled many more women to assume leadership positions or facilitated a recognition and celebration of a range of approaches to leadership among women. No matter to what lengths women go to conceal womanliness, it remains obvious and incriminating to those who are bestowing, or refraining from bestowing, the status of leader. Denial of gender is not a strategy that is rewarded with leadership; but neither do women and leadership go together without requiring special designation as the exception to the rule.

These are substantial hurdles indeed to doing leadership differently. They are deeply embedded in cultural mythology, in economic structures and in social expectations. And they are reinforced in, and largely unquestioned by, the substantial annals of leadership theory.

Prospects for Change

Can we be hopeful about change, given these obstacles? Despite often feeling impatient, occasionally desolate, at lost opportunities for change, the conclusion I reach in the final part of the book is that the obstacles are not insurmountable. Change *is* possible, and there is some cause for optimism. The encouraging evidence is of two kinds. The first comes from examining the impact of legislative and structural reforms on workplaces. For example, there are now many more women in the workforce and many more at middle levels of organisations; young women are strongly represented in formerly male-dominated professions such as engineering and science, and women themselves now confidently expect to be able to have families and not prematurely end their careers. If we step back from the frustrations and disappointments of individual experiences and take a longer-term and wider view, we can indeed see evidence of significant shifts in opportunities for leadership available to women.

The second sort of evidence of change has been the subject of this book. It comes from individual women and men who in different ways are bringing new and previously censored parts of themselves into their workplaces and into the way they lead. Their processes of self-examination, experimentation and pushing boundaries have been fostered by many things. Social and legislative change, the emergence of the dual-career couple and the dual-income household as a norm, and women's increased earning power have reconstructed expectations in younger men and women about what their careers and lives will look like.

Feminism has give women a way of understanding that their experiences of discrimination are not 'their fault'. Women's

initiatives on many fronts—in business, the professions, the bureaucracy, voluntary and entrepreneurial ventures—have shown other
women how to have confidence in their abilities and to organise.
Women have also learned how to take collectively based, institutional
and political actions which expand opportunities while directly and
indirectly reducing the incidence of discrimination. These are lessons
which men's groups and those concerned about the future of boys are
just beginning to emulate.

Men's ways of working and leading have also been changed by
social, economic and cultural trends. Popular discussion of men's
issues, from parenting through to reducing the risks of accident and
injury on worksites, has prompted men to explore the costs of how
they work. One of many impacts of the gay movement has been to
expand roles available to men beyond that of 'breadwinner' in a
nuclear family structure, whose energies were expected to be vested
solely in work.

Daily encounters with women and with feminism, through
interactions with sisters, mothers, female friends and partners, is
nurturing reflection among men about their values and priorities.
And those encounters are provoking men to question the obstacles
confronted by friends, partners and daughters. In a personal example,
I was struck, after Charlie was born, by how my youngish male
obstetrician made his post-natal visits to the hospital in his jeans and
with his seven-year-old daughter. When my older children were
born, the obstetrician was only ever seen in a suit across a desk, or
shrouded in the mystique of surgical gown.

But while change is possible and even likely, it will not occur
without resistance and conflict. Many people have much at stake in
maintaining the status quo. And beyond the entrenched power and
interests ranged against change, there are unconscious forces at
work. I have argued that the sexualisation of women in organisations
and the maternalisation of women in authority reveal the extent of
fear of the feminine in the public domain. These processes will continue to be powerful and effective vehicles to undermine, ridicule
and demonise female leaders.

Although there is no simple antidote to these obstacles, we do
know that describing and discussing such complex phenomena can

help to move them out of the unconscious and make them more accessible to considered review. Female leaders are seen differently, judged against buried maternal ideals and likely to evoke fears such as dependency. In contrast, the enactment of leadership by males is likely to start out, at least, as familiar, if not reassuring. A fuller understanding of leadership requires recognition of these fundamental relationships between gender, sexuality and leading.

Some social and cultural factors are moving us towards change in patterns of gender relations and leadership, while other economic and cultural factors constrain change. Structural changes in the economy have resulted in women being a growing component of the workforce, with women finding employment more easily than their partners (albeit at lower pay and casualised conditions). These circumstances are having profound effects on men. Men who have traditionally built an identity, and a life, around work and their role as primary breadwinner are likely to respond defensively to changes in workplaces. For some, a pre-existing ambivalence about women with authority is magnified under conditions of economic uncertainty and in the cultural turbulence of postmodern multicultural Australia.

It is probably impossible and certainly unwise to conclude by predicting when and how various forces will coalesce into a change in Australian leadership. Instead we need to look beyond theoretical prescriptions and into the practices, and lives, of individual leaders. Here we find many women and men who are doing leadership differently—working to change experiences and expectations about who leaders are and what they should do. With them there is cause for celebration and hope for the future.

BIBLIOGRAPHY

Adler, N. (1993) 'Asian Women in Management' *International Studies of Management and Organization* 23(4): 3–17.

────── (1996) 'Global Women in History: An Invisible History, an Increasingly Important Future' *Leadership Quarterly* 7(1): 133–71.

Adler, N. and Izraeli, D. (eds) (1988) *Women in Management Worldwide* New York: M. E. Sharpe.

────── (1993) *Competitive Frontiers: Women Managers in a Global Economy* Cambridge, Mass.: Blackwell.

Alderfer, C. and Smith, K. (1982) 'Studying Intergroup Relations Embedded in Organizations' *Administrative Science Quarterly* 27: 35–65.

Bagwell, S. (1992) 'The Door is Ajar' *Business Review Weekly* 12 June: 43–7.

Barrett, F. (1996) 'The Organizational Construction of Hegemonic Masculinity: The Case of the U.S. Navy' *Gender, Work and Organization* 3(3): 129–42.

Bass, B. and Stogdill, R. (1990, 3rd edn) *Bass and Stogdill's Handbook of Leadership: Theory, Research and Managerial Applications* New York: The Free Press.

Baum, H. (1987) *The Invisible Bureaucracy* New York: Oxford University Press.

Bayes, M. and Newton, P. (1978) 'Women in Authority: A Socio-psychological Analysis' *Journal of Applied Behavioural Science* 14: 7–20.

Belenky, M., Clinchy, B., Goldberger, N. and Tarule, J. (1986) *Women's Ways of Knowing: The Development of Self, Voice and Mind* New York: Basic Books.

Bellamy, P. and Ramsay, K. (1994) *Barriers to Women Working in Corporate Management* Canberra: Australian Government Publishing Service.

Bem, S. (1974) 'The Measurement of Psychological Androgyny' *Journal of Consulting and Clinical Psychology* 42(2): 155–62.

―――― (1981) 'Gender Schema Theory: A Cognitive Account of Sex Typing' *Psychological Review* 88(4): 354–64.

Bennis, W. and Nanus, B. (1985) *Leaders: The Strategies of Taking Charge* New York: Harper & Row.

Berdahl, J. (1996) 'Gender and Leadership in Work Groups: Six Alternative Models' *Leadership Quarterly* (7)1: 21–40.

Betz, N. (1994) 'Basic Issues and Concepts in Career Counselling for Women' in W. Walsh and S. Osipow (eds) *Career Counselling for Women* New Jersey: Lawrence Erlbaum Assoc.

Betz, N. and Fitzgerald, L. (1987) *The Career Psychology of Women* Orlando, Florida: Harcourt Brace.

Biddulph, S. (1994) *Manhood* Sydney: Finch.

―――― (1997) *Raising Boys* Sydney: Finch.

Blum, L. and Smith, V. (1988) 'Women's Mobility in the Corporation: A Critique of the Politics of Optimism' *Signs: Journal of Women in Culture and Society* 13(3): 528–45.

Bly, R. (1990) *Iron John: A Book about Men* Reading, Mass.: Addison Wesley.

Bourdieu, P. and Boltanski, L. (1978) 'Changes in Social Structure and Changes in the Demand for Education' in S. Giner and M. Archer (eds) *Contemporary Europe: Social Structure and Cultural Patterns* London: Routledge.

Bourdieu, P. and Passeron, J. (1977) *Reproduction in Education, Society and Culture* (trans. R. Nice) London: Sage.

Bremmer, O., Tomkiewicz, J. and Schein, V. (1989) 'The Relationship between Sex-role Stereotypes and Requisite Managerial Characteristics Revisited' *Academy of Management Journal* 32(3): 662–9.

Brett, J. (1996) 'Gunning for the All-Australian Macho Image' *Age* 10 May: A15.

Brett, J. (ed.) (1997) *Political Lives* Sydney: Allen & Unwin.

Burke, R. and McKeen, C. (1996) 'Do Women at the Top Make a Difference? Gender Proportions and the Experiences of Managerial and Professional Women' *Human Relations* 49(8): 1093–104.

Burns, J. (1978) *Leadership* New York: Harper & Row.

Burrell, G. (1984) 'Sex and Organizational Analysis' *Organization Studies* 5(2): 97–118.

—— (1987) 'No Accounting for Sexuality' *Accounting, Organizations and Society* 12(1): 89–101.

Burrell, G. and Hearn, J. (1989) 'The Sexuality of Organization' in J. Hearn *et al. The Sexuality of Organization* London: Sage.

Burton, C. (1991) *The Promise and the Price* Sydney: Allen & Unwin.

Calas, M. and Smircich, L. (1991) 'Voicing Seduction to Silence Leadership' *Organization Studies* 12(4): 567–601.

Cameron, P. (1997) *Finishing School for Blokes* Sydney: Allen & Unwin.

Carruthers, F. (1997) 'Women Lose Battle of the Boardrooms' *Australian* 8–9 February: 1, 6.

Chodorow, N. (1979) *The Reproduction of Mothering* Berkeley Calif.: University of California Press.

—— (1994) *Femininities, Masculinities, Sexualities: Freud and Beyond* London: Free Association Books.

Coates, J. (1996) *Women Talk* Oxford: Blackwell.

Cockburn, C. (1983) *Brothers: Male Dominance and Technological Change* London: Pluto Press.

—— (1985) *Machinery of Dominance: Women, Men and Technological Know-How* London: Pluto Press.

—— (1990) 'Men's Power in Organizations: "Equal Opportunities" Intervenes' in J. Hearn and D. Morgan (eds) *Men, Masculinities and Social Theory* London: Unwin Hyman.

—— (1991) *In the Way of Women: Men's Resistance to Sex Equality in Organizations* London: Macmillan.

Collinson, D. (1992) *Managing the Shopfloor: Subjectivity, Masculinity and Workplace Culture* Berlin: De Gruyter.

Collinson, D. and Hearn, J. (1994) 'Naming Men as Men: Implications for Work, Organization and Management' *Gender, Work and Organization* 1(1): 2–22.

—— (1996) *Men as Managers, Managers as Men: Critical Perspectives on Men, Masculinities and Managements* London: Sage.

Collinson, D., Knights, D. and Collinson, M. (1990) *Managing to Discriminate* London: Routledge.

Connell, R. (1987) *Gender and Power: Society, the Person and Sexual Politics* Cambridge: Polity Press.

—— (1995) *Masculinities* Sydney: Allen & Unwin.

—— (1995) Interview in the *Age* 31 May.

Court, M. (1995) 'Good Girls and Naughty Girls: Rewriting the Scripts for Women's Anger' in B. Limerick and B. Lingard (eds) *Gender and Changing Educational Management* Sydney: Hodder.

Cox, E. (1996) *Leading Women: Tactics for Making the Difference* Sydney: Random House.

Cox, T. (1993) *Cultural Diversity in Organizations* San Francisco: Berret-Koehler.

Cox, T. and Blake, S. (1991) 'Managing Cultural Diversity: Implications for Organizational Competitiveness' *Academy of Management Executive* 5(3): 45–54.

Creed, B. (1993) *The Monstrous Feminine: Film, Feminism, Psychoanalysis* London: Routledge.

Dagher, J. and D'Netto, B. (1997) *Managing Workforce Diversity in Australia* Monash University Department of Management Working Paper 5/97.

Dainty, P. and Anderson, M. (1996) *The Capable Executive: Effective Performance in Senior Management* London: Macmillan.

Davidson, M. and Cooper, C. (1992) *Shattering the Glass Ceiling: The Woman Manager* London: Paul Chapman.

de Beauvoir, S. (1953) *The Second Sex* London: Jonathan Cape.

Denhardt, R. (1981) *In the Shadow of Organization*, Lawrence: Regents Press of Kansas.

Dessaix, R. (1994) *A Mother's Disgrace* Sydney: Angus and Robertson.

Dinnerstein, D. (1978) *The Rocking of the Cradle: And the Ruling of the World* London: Souvenir Press.

Di Stefano, C. (1991) *Configurations of Masculinity: A Feminist Perspective on Modern Political Theory* Ithaca, NY: Cornell University Press.

Dobrzynski, J. (1996) 'Women Pass Milestone in Boardroom' *New York Times* 12 December.

Doogue, G. (1995) Interview with Rick Farley *Radio National* 12 May.

Dowling, P. and Nagel, T. (1986) 'Nationality and Work Attitudes: A Study of Australian and American Business Majors' *Journal of Management* 12(1): 121–8.

Eagly, A. (1992) 'Gender and the Evaluation of Leaders' *Psychological Bulletin* 111(1): 3–22.

Eagly, A. and Johnson, B. (1990) 'Gender and Leadership Style: A Meta-analysis' *Psychological Bulletin* 108(2): 233–56.

Egon Zehnder Australia and Melbourne Business School (1997) *Corporate Governance and Globalising Business: Reconciling Competing Pressures* Melbourne: Egon Zehnder S. A.

Ely, R. (1995) 'The Power in Demography: Women's Social Construction of Gender Identity at Work *Academy of Management Journal* 38(3): 589–634.

Eveline, J. (1994) 'The Politics of Advantage' *Australian Feminist Studies* 19 (August): 129–54.

—— (1996) 'The Worry of Going Limp: Are You Keeping Up in Senior Management' *Australian Feminist Studies* 11(3): 65–79.

Foucault, M. (1981) *The History of Sexuality* Vol. 1, London: Penguin.

French, K. (1995) 'Men and Locations of Power. Why Move Over?' in C. Itzin and J. Newman *Gender, Culture and Organizational Change: Putting Theory into Practice* London: Routledge.

Freud, A. (1936/37) *The Ego and the Mechanisms of Defence* (trans. C. Baines) London: The Hogarth Press/Institute of Psycho-analysis (fifth impression 1961).

Gibson, C. (1995) 'An Investigation of Gender Differences in Leadership Across Four Countries' *Journal of International Business Studies* 26(2): 255–79.

Gilligan, C. (1977) 'Concepts of the Self and Morality' *Harvard Educational Review* 47(4): 481–517.

—— (1982) *In a Different Voice: Psychological Theory and Women's Development*. Cambridge, Mass.: Harvard University Press.

Gilligan, C., Ward, J., Taylor, J. and Bardige, B. (eds) (1988) *Mapping the Moral Domain: A Contribution of Women's Thinking to Psychological Theory and Education* Cambridge, Mass.: Centre for the Study of

Gender, Education and Human Development, Harvard University.

Gilmore, D. (1990) *Manhood in the Making: Cultural Concepts of Masculinity* New Haven, Conn.: Yale University Press.

Glass Ceiling Commission (1995) *A Solid Investment: Making Full Use of the Nation's Human Capital* Washington: US Government Printing Office

Goffee, R. and Scase, R. (1985) *Women in Charge: The Experience of Female Entrepreneurs* London: Allen & Unwin.

Gordon, S. (1991) *Prisoners of Men's Dreams: Striking Out for a New Feminine Future* Boston: Little, Brown.

Grieve, N. and Perdices, M. (1981) 'Patriarchy: A Refuge from Maternal Power? in N. Grieve and P. Grimshaw (eds) *Australian Women: Feminist Perspectives* Melbourne: Oxford University Press.

Gronn, P. (1995) 'Greatness Revisited: The Current Obsession with Transformational Leadership' *Leading and Managing* 1(1): 14–27.

Gutek, B. (1985) *Sex and the Workplace: Impact of Sexual Behavior and Harassment on Women, Men and Organizations* San Francisco: Jossey Bass.

—— (1993) 'Changing the Status of Women in Management' *Applied Psychology: An International Review* 42(4): 301–11.

Gutek, B., Cohen, A. and Tsui, A. (1996) 'Reactions to Perceived Sex Discrimination' *Human Relations* 49(6): 791–813.

Gutek, B. and Morasch, B. (1982) 'Sex Ratios, Sex-role Spillover and Sexual Harassment of Women at Work' *Journal of Social Issues* 38: 58–74.

Hampden-Turner, C. and Trompenaars, A. (1993) *The Seven Cultures of Capitalism: Value Systems for Creating Wealth in the United States, Japan, Germany, France, Britain, Sweden and the Netherlands.* New York: Doubleday.

Handy, C. (1989) *The Age of Unreason* London: Penguin Business Books.

Hay, C. (1996) *Managing Cultural Diversity* A Report for the Bureau of Immigration, Population, and Multiculturalism Melbourne: Australian Government Publishing Service.

Hearn, J. (1992) 'Changing Men and Changing Managements' *Women in Management Review* 7(1): 3–8.

Hearn, J. and Morgan, D. (eds) (1990) *Men, Masculinities and Social Theory* London: Unwin Hyman.

Hearn, J. and Parkin, W. (1987) *'Sex' at 'Work': The Power and Paradox of Organizational Sexuality* Brighton, UK: Wheatsheaf.

Hearn, J., Sheppard, D., Tancred-Sherif, P. and Burrell, G. (1989) *The Sexuality of Organization* London: Sage.

Helgesen, S. (1990) *Female Advantage: Women's Ways of Leadership* New York: Doubleday.

Henderson, G. (1994) *Cultural Diversity in the Workplace: Issues and Strategies* Westport, Conn.: Quorum Books.

Hochschild, A. (1997) *The Time Bind: When Work Becomes Home and Home Becomes Work* New York: Metropolitan Books.

Hofstede, G. (1980) *Culture's Consequences: International Differences in Work-related Values* Beverly Hills, Calif.: Sage.

—— (1991) *Cultures and Organizations: Softwares of the Mind* Berkshire, UK: McGraw Hill.

Hofstede, G., Neuijen, B., Ohayv, D. and Sanders, G. (1990) 'Measuring Organizational Cultures: A Qualitative and Quantitative Study Across Twenty Cases *Administrative Science Quarterly* 35(2): 283–316.

Holton, L. (1995) 'Women on the Boards of Britain's Top 200 Companies' *Women in Management Review* 10(3): 16–20.

—— (1996) reviews of *The Female Advantage* and *Women World Leaders* in *Occupational Psychologist* 30: 56–9.

Hoojiberg, R. and DiTomaso, N. (1996) 'Leadership In and Of Demographically Diverse Organisations' *Leadership Quarterly* (7)1: 1–20.

Horner, M. (1972) 'Toward an Understanding of Achievement Related Conflicts in Women' *Journal of Social Issues* 2(2): 157–75.

Hummel, R. P. (1982, 2nd edn) *The Bureaucratic Experience* New York: St. Martin's Press.

Hunt, J. (1995) *Executive Development and Leadership Report: Key Components in the Development of Senior Executives in Australia* report published by Excelsior Pacific Management Consultants, Sydney.

Hunt, J., Hosking, D., Schriesheim, C. and Stewart, R. (1984) *Leaders and Managers: International Perspectives on Managerial Behaviour and Leadership* New York: Pergamon.

Hunter, F. and Reid, T. (1996) 'The Power Game: Do Women Make Better Bosses?' *Sunday Telegraph* (UK) 3 November.

Ibarra, H. (1995) 'Race, Opportunity and Diversity of Social Circles in Managerial Networks', *Academy of Management Journal* 38(3): 673–703.

Illich, I. (1982) *Gender* New York: Pantheon Books.

Industry Taskforce on Leadership and Management Skills (1995) *Enterprising Nation: Renewing Australia's Managers to Meet the Challenges of the Asia-Pacific Century* (also known as The Karpin Report) Canberra: Australian Government Publishing Service.

Irigaray, L. (1993) *An Ethics of Sexual Difference* London: Athlone.

Iseman, K. (1981) 'Our Fathers' Daughters: The Problem of Filiation for Women Writers of Fiction' in N. Grieve and P. Grimshaw (eds) *Australian Women: Feminist Perspectives* Melbourne: Oxford University Press.

Itzin, C. and Newman, J. (1995) *Gender, Culture and Organizational Change: Putting Theory into Practice* London: Routledge.

James, D. (1996) 'Managing: Big Stick Approach gets Caning from the Floor' *Business Review Weekly* 20 May: 164–5.

Jung, C. G. (1968 2nd edn) *The Archetypes and the Collective Unconscious* (trans. by R. F. Hull) Bollinger Series XX, Princeton, NJ: Princeton University Press (first published 1934).

Kanter, R. (1977) *Men and Women of the Corporation* New York: Basic Books.

——— (1979) 'Power Failure in Management Circuits' *Harvard Business Review* 57(4), July–August: 65–75.

Karpin, D. (1994) 'Glass Ceiling: Illusory or Real?' Proceedings of a Conference on Women, Organisations and Economic Policies, Canberra. Reproduced in *Canberra Bulletin of Public Administration* 76: 67–70.

Karston, M. (1994) *Management and Gender: Issues and Attitudes* Westport, Conn.: Quorum Books.

Kerfoot, D. and Knights, D. (1993) 'Management, Masculinity and Manipulation: From Paternalism to Corporate Strategy in Financial Services in Britain' *Journal of Management Studies* 30(4): 659–78.

Kets de Vries, M. (1988) ' Prisoners of Leadership' *Human Relations*, 41:3: 261–80.

——— (1996) 'The Anatomy of the Entrepreneur: Clinical Observations *Human Relations* 47(9): 853–83.

Kets de Vries, M. and Miller, D. (1984) *The Neurotic Organization* San Francisco: Jossey Bass.

Kimmel, M. (1990) 'After Fifteen Years: The Impact of the Sociology of Masculinity on the Masculinity of Sociology' in J. Hearn and D. Morgan (eds) *Men, Masculinities and Social Theory* London: Unwin Hyman.

Kimmel, M. (ed.) (1995) *The Politics of Manhood: Profeminist Men Respond to the Mythopoetic Men's Movement* Philadelphia: Temple University Press.

Kirkman, M. and Grieve, N. (1984) 'Women, Power and Ordination: A Psychological Interpretation of Objections to the Ordination of Women to the Priesthood' *Women's Studies International Forum* 7(6): 487–94.

Kirkpatrick, S. and Locke, E. (1991) 'Leadership: Do Traits Matter?' *Academy of Management Executive* 5(2): 48–59.

Korn Ferry International (1993) *Decade of the Executive Woman* New York: Korn Ferry International.

Kotter, J. (1986) 'Why Power and Influence are at the Very Core of Executive Work' in S. Srivastva & Assoc. (eds) *Executive Power* San Francisco: Jossey Bass.

——— (1988) *The Leadership Factor* New York: The Free Press.

——— (1990) *A Force for Change: How Leadership Differs from Management* New York: The Free Press.

LaBier, D. (1984) 'Irrational Behaviour in Bureaucracy' in M. F. R. Kets de Vries (ed.) *The Irrational Executive* New York: International Universities Press: 3–37.

Lacan, J. (1966) *Feminine Sexuality* (J. Mitchell and J. Rose eds) New York: Norton.

Lake, M. (1986) 'The Politics of Respectability: Identifying the Masculinist Contest' *Historical Studies* 22: 116–31.

——— (1995) 'Birth of History' *Weekend Australian* 18 / 19 March: 26.

Landau, J. (1995) 'The Relationship of Race and Gender to Managers' Ratings of Promotional Potential' *Journal of Organizational Behavior* 16: 395–400.

Larriera, A. (1996) 'Women Overlooked in Top Overseas Postings: Study' *Age* 9 December.

Lasswell, H. D. (1930) *Psychopathology and Politics* Chicago: University of Chicago Press.

Lauterbach, K. and Weiner, B. (1996) 'Dynamics of Upward Influence: How Male and Female Managers Get Their Way' *Leadership Quarterly* 7(1): 87–108.

Levant, R. (1995) *Masculinity Reconstructed* New York: Dutton.

Linstead, S. (1995) 'Averting the Gaze: Gender and Power on the Perfumed Picket Line' *Gender, Work and Organization* 2(4): 192–206.

Little, G. (1985) *Political Ensembles: A Psychosocial Approach to Politics and Leadership* Melbourne: Oxford University Press.

—— (1988) *Strong Leadership* Melbourne: Oxford University Press.

Liverani, M. (1995) 'Gender Bias and Women Working in the Legal System' *Law Society Journal* May: 32–6.

Lobel, S. (1993) 'Sexuality at Work: Where Do We Go from Here?' *Journal of Vocational Behavior* 42: 136–52.

Loden, M. (1985) *Feminine Leadership or How to Succeed in Business Without Being One of the Boys* New York: Time Books.

Loden, M. and Rosener, J. (1991) *Workforce America! Managing Employee Diversity as a Vital Resource* Homewood, Ill.: Irwin Business.

Lukes, S. (1974) *Power: A Radical View* London: Macmillan.

McKenna, E. P. (1997) *When Work Doesn't Work Anymore: Women, Work and Identity* Sydney: Hodder Headline.

Maddock, S. and Parkin, S. (1993) 'Gender Cultures: Women's Choices and Strategies at Work' *Women in Management Review* 8(2): 3–9.

Maier, M. (1997) 'Gender, Equity, Organizational Transformation and Challenger' *Journal of Business Ethics* 16(9): 943–62.

Mant, A. (1983) *Leaders We Deserve* Oxford: Basil Blackwell.

Marshall, Judi (1984) *Women Managers: Travellers in a Male World* Chichester UK: Wiley.

—— (1991) 'Women Managers' in A. Mumford (ed.) *Gower Handbook of Management Development* (3rd edn) Aldershot UK: Gower.

—— (1993a) 'Organisational Cultures and Women Managers: Exploring the Dynamics of Resilience' *Applied Psychology: An International Review* 42(4) 313–22.

—— (1993b) 'Viewing Organizational Communication from a Feminist Perspective: A Critique and Some Offerings' in S. Deetz (ed.) *Communication Yearbook* Vol. 16, Newbury Park, Calif.: Sage.

—— (1995a) *Women Managers Moving On: Exploring Life and Career Choices* London: Routledge.

—— (1995b) 'Working at Senior Management and Board Levels' *Women in Management Review* 10(3): 21–5.

Maupin, R. and Lehman, C. (1994) 'Talking Heads: Stereotypes, Status, Sex-roles and Satisfaction of Female and Male Auditors' *Accounting, Organizations and Society* 19(4/5): 427–37.

Meindl, J., Ehrlich, S. and Dukerich, J. (1985) 'The Romance of Leadership' *Administrative Science Quarterly* 30: 78–102.

Menadue, J. (1996) 'Cross-cultural Differences in Asia-Pacific: The Catalyst for Organisational Change' *Management Consultants 1996 World Conference* Yokahama, Japan, 10–12 September.

Mitchell, J. (1975) *Psychoanalysis and Feminism* Harmondsworth: Penguin.

—— (1982) 'Introduction' in *Feminine Sexuality: Jacques Lacan and the Ecole Freudienne* New York: Norton.

Mitchell, S. (1996) *The Scent of Power* Sydney: Angus and Robertson.

Morrison, A. (1992) *The New Leaders: Guidelines on Leadership Diversity in America* San Francisco: Jossey Bass.

Mulholland, K. (1996) 'Entrepreneurialism, Masculinities and the Self-Made Man', in D. Collinson and J. Hearn (eds) *Men as Managers, Managers as Men* London: Sage.

Neales, S. (1996) 'Rick Farley Quits the Rat Race' *Age Good Weekend Magazine* 24 August: 22–7.

Nieva, V. and Gutek, B. (1981) *Women and Work: A Psychological Perspective* Praeger: New York

Norton, J. (1991) 'My Love, She Speaks Like Silence: Men, Sex and Subjectivity' *Melbourne Journal of Politics* 20: 148–88.

—— (1997) 'Deconstructing the Fear of Femininity' *Feminism and Psychology* 7(3): 443–9.

Office of Multicultural Affairs (1993) *Australian Business and Cultural Diversity* Canberra: Australian Government Publishing Service.

Parkin, D. and Maddock, S. (1995) 'A Gender Typology of Organizational Culture' in C. Itzin and J. Newman *Gender, Culture and Organizational Change: Putting Theory into Practice* London: Routledge.

Pfeffer, J. (1992) *Managing with Power: Politics and Influence in Organizations* Boston: Harvard Business School Press.

Poole, M. and Langan-Fox, J. (1997) *Australian Women and Career: Psychological and Contextual Influences Over the Life Course* Cambridge: Cambridge University Press.

Porter, P. (1994) 'Women and Leadership in Education: The Construction of Gender in the Workplace' 1994 Buntine Oration, published as Occasional Paper 23, Australian College of Education.

Powell, G. (1988) *Women and Men in Management* Beverly Hills, Calif.: Sage.

—— (1990) 'One More Time: Do Female and Male Managers Differ? *Academy of Management Executive* 4: 68–74.

Pringle, J. (1996) 'Transgendering Management: Issues and Impacts of Women in Management Research' paper delivered at Aust. and New Zealand Academy of Management Conference, Wollongong, December.

Pringle, R. (1988) *Secretaries Talk: Sexuality, Power and Work* Sydney: Allen & Unwin.

—— (1992) 'Absolute Sex? Unpacking the Sexuality/Gender Relationship' in R. Connell and G. Dowsett (eds) *Rethinking Sex: Social Theory and Sexuality Research* Melbourne: Melbourne University Press.

Redwood, Rene (1996) Speech to the American Chamber of Commerce in Australia, Melbourne, December.

Riger, S. and Galligan, P. (1980) 'Women in Management: An Exploration of Competing Paradigms' *American Psychologist* 35(10): 902–10.

Roper, M. (1994) *Masculinity and the British Organization Man Since 1945* Oxford: Oxford University Press.

———— (1996) 'Seduction and Succession: Circuits of Homosocial Desire in Management' in D. Collinson and J. Hearn (eds) *Men as Managers, Managers as Men* London: Sage.

Roper, M. and Tosh, J. (eds) (1991) *Manful Assertions: Masculinities in Britain since 1800* London: Routledge.

Rosener, J. (1990) 'Ways Women Lead' *Harvard Business Review* November–December, 68(6): 119–25.

———— (1995) *America's Competitive Secret: Women Managers* New York: Oxford University Press.

Sarney, E. (1997) 'Girls on Top' *New Zealand Sunday Star Times* 2 February: E1.

Sarros, J. (1991) *The Executives* Melbourne: Lothian.

Sarros, J. and Butchasky, O. (1996) *Leadership: Australia's Top CEOs: Finding Out What Makes Them the Best* Sydney: Harper Business.

Saunders, H. (1996) *Acts of Courage? Public Sector CEOs on Men, Women and Work* Perth: Director of Equal Opportunity in Public Employment.

Schein, V. (1973) 'The Relationship Between Sex Role Stereotypes and Requisite Managerial Characteristics' *Journal of Applied Psychology* 57: 95–100.

———— (1975) 'The Relationship Between Sex-Role Stereotypes and Requisite Managerial Characteristics' *Journal of Applied Psychology* 60: 340–4.

Schein, V., Mueller, R., Lituchy, T. and J. Liu (1996) 'Think Manager—Think Male: A Global Phenomenon?' *Journal of Organizational Behavior* 17: 33–41.

Schwartz, F. (1989) 'Management Women and the New Facts of Life' *Harvard Business Review* January–February: 65–76.

Sheehy, G. (1994) *New Passages* New York: Basic Books.

Sheppard, D. (1989) 'Organizations, Power and Sexuality: The Image and Self-image of Women Managers' in J. Hearn, D. Sheppard, P. Tancred-Sherif and G. Burrell *The Sexuality of Organization* London: Sage.

Shope, D. (1975) *Interpersonal Sexuality* Philadelphia: W. B. Saunders & Co.

Sinclair, A. (1987) *Getting the Numbers: Women in Local Government* Melbourne: Hargreen/Municipal Association of Victoria.

—— (1990) *Archetypes of Leadership* Graduate School of Management Working Paper 11, Melbourne.

—— (1994) *Trials at the Top* Melbourne: Australian Centre, University of Melbourne.

—— (1995a) 'Sex and the MBA' *Organization* 2(2): 295–317.

—— (1995b) 'Sexuality in Leadership' *International Review of Women in Leadership* 1(2): 25–38.

—— (1995c) 'The Chameleon of Accountability: Forms and Discourses' *Accounting, Organizations and Society* 19(2): 219–37.

—— (1995d) *Gender in the Management Curriculum* Melbourne: Equal Employment Opportunity Unit, University of Melbourne.

—— (1995e) 'The Seduction of the Self-Managed Team' *Leading and Managing* 1(1): 44–62.

—— (1996a) 'Leadership in Administration' in G. Davis and P. Weller *New Ideas, Better Government* Sydney: Allen & Unwin.

—— (1996b) *Journey Without Maps: Transforming Management Education* Inaugural Professorial Lecture, Melbourne Business School, University of Melbourne.

Smith, B. (1995) *Mothers and Sons* Sydney: Allen & Unwin.

Smith, C. and Hutchinson, J. (1995) *Gender: A Strategic Management Issue* Sydney: Business and Professional Publishing.

Smith, C. and Still, L. (1996) 'Gender Diversity in International Assignments: The Australian Experience' Paper delivered to the 10th Anniversary Conference of the Australian and New Zealand Academy of Management, Wollongong, 4–7 December 1996.

Still, L. (1993) *Where To From Here? The Managerial Woman in Transition* Sydney: Business and Professional Publishing.

Stivers, C. (1993) *Gender Images in Public Administration: Legitimacy and the Administrative State* Newbury Park, Calif.: Sage.

—— (1996) 'Mary Parker Follett and the Question of Gender' *Organization* 3(1): 161–6.

Stogdill, R. (1948) 'Personal Factors Associated with Leadership': A Survey of the Literature' *Journal of Psychology* 25: 64.

—— (1974) *Handbook of Leadership* New York: Free Press.

Stroh, L., Brett, J. and Reilly, A. (1992) 'All the Right Stuff: A Comparison of Female and Male Managers' Career Progression' *Journal of Applied Psychology* 77(3): 251–60.

Super, D. and Sverko, B. (eds) (1995) *Life Roles, Values and Careers: International Findings of the Work Importance Study* San Francisco: Jossey Bass.

Swan, Elaine (1994) 'Managing Emotion' in M. Tanton (ed.) *Women in Management: A Developing Presence* London: Routledge.

Swan, N. (1996) Interview with Daniel Petrie *Radio National* 26 September.

Tacey, D. (1995) 'The Rites and Wrongs of Passage: Drugs, Gangs, Suicides, Gurus' *Psychotherapy in Australia* 1(4): 5–12.

—— (1997) *Remaking Men* Harmondsworth: Viking.

Tharenou, P., Latimer, S. and Conroy, D. (1994) 'How Do You Make It to the Top? An Examination of Influences on Women's and Men's Managerial Advancement *Academy of Management Journal* 37(4): 899–931.

Thomas, R. (1996) *Redefining Diversity* New York: AMACOM.

Tolson, A. (1977) *The Limits of Masculinity* London: Tavistock.

Tsui, A., Egan, T. and O'Reilly, C. (1992) 'Being Different: Relational Demography and Organizational Attachment' *Administrative Science Quarterly* 37: 549–79.

University of Western Australia *Leadership Development Program for Women: Interim Report* November 1995.

Watson, C. and Hoffman, L. (1996) 'Managers as Negotiators: A Test of Power versus Gender as Predictors of Feelings, Behavior, and Outcomes' *Leadership Quarterly* 7(1): 63–86.

Watson, I. (1996) *Opening the Glass Door: Overseas-born Managers in Australia* A Report for the Bureau of Immigration, Multicultural and Population Research, Canberra: Australian Government Publishing Service.

Weiner, G. (1995) 'A Question of Style or Value? Contrasting Perceptions of Women as Educational Leaders' in B. Limerick and B. Lingard (eds) *Gender and Changing Educational Management* Sydney: Hodder.

White, J. (1995) 'Leading in their Own Ways: Women Chief Executives in Local Government' in C. Itzin and J. Newman *Gender, Culture and Organizational Change: Putting Theory into Practice* London: Routledge.

Wilson, F. (1995) *Organisational Behaviour and Gender* London: McGraw Hill.

Winton, T. (1994) 'The Masculine Mystique' *Age Good Weekend* 27 August: 61–7.

Woodward, A. (1996) 'Multinational Masculinities and European Bureaucracies' in D. Collinson and J. Hearn (eds), *Men as Managers, Managers as Men* London: Sage: 167–85.

Wright, P., Ferris, S., Hiller, J. and Kroll, M. (1995) 'Competitiveness through Management of Diversity' *Academy of Management Journal* 38(1): 272–87.

Xin, K. and Tsui, A. (1996) 'Different Strokes for Different Folks? Influence Tactics by Asian–American and Caucasian–American Managers' *Leadership Quarterly* (7)1: 109–32.

Zaleznik, A. (1977) 'Managers and Leaders: Are they Different' *Harvard Business Review* 55(2): 67–78.

INDEX

compiled by Geraldine Suter

and sons, 67, 70–2 *passim*, 74;
influence on daughters, 77, 80–3,
89–90; Steve Biddulph's work, 67,
148, 150
fear of the feminine, 56, 131, 137–8
female influence strategies, 108–28;
and consultation, 107, 110–11,
122, 126–7, 139; and sexuality,
109, 167–9; avoiding slanging
matches, 114, 124–5; being a confidante, 113, 117–18, 165–6; creating professional/industry profile,
113–15, 128; derivation, 125–8;
gender differences, 109–12, 128;
networking, 113–14, 119, 120,
169; persistence and professionalism, 113–14, 118–19; private/
professional boundaries, 113–14,
122–4, 128, 168, 171–2; submerging ego, 113–17; surprise,
shock and challenge, 113–14,
119–20; team building, 114,
120–2
female leaders, backgrounds of: born
v. made, 78–80; childhood hardships, 77, 80, 88–9, 90; early years,
77–92; female role models, 85–7;
insulation from gender stereotyping, 77–8, 80, 89; parental influences, 77, 80–2
female leadership: origins of concepts
of, 28–30; reluctance to label selves
as leaders, 10, 95–6, 105–7; underplay leadership role, 12, 92, 94–6,
106–7, 114; viewed as different,
16–17; *see also* Absence Argument;
female influence strategies; female
sexuality; Invisibility Argument;
power, obstacles to women
female mentors and role models, 18;
ambivalence of female leaders, 21,
121, 127–8; being a confidante, 87,
113, 117–18, 165–6; role models,
83–7 *passim*, 90–1, 103–4, 112; *see
also* tokenism

female sexuality, 80; and self-esteem,
161–2; defined, 157–8; denial/
high power, 166–8; denial/low
power, 164–5; high awareness/high
power, 168–72; high awareness/
low power, 165–6; in leadership,
161–3; model of sexuality and
power, 163–72 *passim*, 176; sexual
affairs, 158, 165; *see also* sex-role
stereotyping
femininity: fear of the feminine, 56,
131, 137–8; sense of self, 60; ter-
minology, 161; women's ways of
knowing, 18; *see also* female sexuality; sex-role stereotyping; sex roles
feminism, 55–6, 60, 61, 157–8, 161
financial services industry, 63–4, 102,
143, 159, 160
formal power, 108, 110
Foucault, M., 157
French, A., 147
Freud, A., 139

Galligan, P., 17, 132
Gates, W., 70, 71
gay and lesbian studies, 56–7
gay men, 42, 46, 56–7, 72, 131, 136
gender difference, 113–14, 122–4; as
biological, 17–18, 145; differential
judgements of same behaviours, 25,
29, 33, 62; in children's play, 126; in
influence strategies, 109–12,
125–6; in leadership, 1–4, 25–6; in
moral thinking, 18, 26, 126; in
motivation, 26; in perception of
need for change, 25, 131, 134–5,
145; in personal power, 108–12;
influence of men's movement, 56;
statistics, 59–60; *see also* sex roles;
sexuality
George, J., 42
Gibson, C., 46, 47
Gilligan, C., 18, 26, 126
glass ceiling, 5–6, 135–6
Glass Ceiling Commission, 5, 135